POWERED TO MOVE

THE MIKE KING STORY

POWERED TO MOVE
THE MIKE KING STORY

Mike King

with Charlynn Johns

2015

Powered to Move

First Printing: 2015, volume 2

ISBN: 978-1-4951-8164-1

Powered to Move
PO Box 1813
Allen, TX 75013

www.poweredtomove.org

Ordering Information:

Special discounts are available on quantity purchases. For details, contact the publisher at the above listed address.

U.S. trade bookstores and wholesalers: Please contact

Powered to Move
484-802-5659
mike@poweredtomove.org

Dedication

My Dad, Paul King, passed away February 10, 2014. His strength instilled in me the determination to never give up. It helped propel my trek across the country in my wheelchair, and is still evident in my life today. He always enjoyed hearing stories of my adventures. This book is dedicated to the legacy of his life that lives on in me, my four brothers, and our familes.

Thank you Pop!

Dad and Mom, without your support, encouragement, and belief in me, I would never have achieved my dreams.

Contents

Acknowledgements

I would like to thank my wife Sharyn, my best friend and love, for your encouragement in writing the continuation of my story; without you and my family (*My Mom;* Dorothy, *Brothers;* Rodney, Curt, Kent and Wendel) this book would not have happened.

Thanks to my friends and family who shared in my adventures. Myron Stoltzfus the brains behind the "*Challenge of a Lifetime.*" The Road Crew: Curt King, James Graybill, Glenn Stoltzfus, Tim Raber, Lauren Martin, Tim Haines, Steve Engle, Lisa Wagner, Teri Shimmer and the entire *Hope for Life* Board for without your support this experience would not have happened.

My friends who pulled me through the early years of being disabled: Myron Stoltzfus, Glen Smoker, Chris Slaybaugh, Jay Embleton and the late Jon Kent Witmer. I will be forever grateful for your words and actions. You showed me I was the same person and friend after my accident.

My friend Sib Charles and the many staff members of *Joni and Friends* who encouraged me to be active in ministry to people affected by disability. You surrounded me with support and direction that guided me to where and who I am today.

My riding buddies on that fateful trip in 1978. Greg Petersheim, thanks for the invitation to join you and Ron and Merv Stoltzfus; tragedy was averted to triumph because of your prayers. Merv passed on from this life but his spirit remains with me in all that we shared.

My Papa Zook, who told my mom, I was going to be okay. Those words reassure me to this day.

A special thanks to Glen Smoker, whose faithfulness to God's voice to contact me about undertaking this project was an answer to prayer. I'm grateful to you my friend and the thousands of lives your obedience will help reach!

I thank God and His Son Jesus Christ for the hope that will forever burn in my heart to live my life to its fullest potential for Him.

Foreword

Before You Begin...

An odd and wonderful mystery occurs in the beginning of Exodus when Moses beholds something totally unnatural. He sees a bush that is on fire, yet is not consumed. "So Moses thought, 'I will go over and see this strange sight — why the bush does not burn up (*Exodus 3:3*).

Christians who suffer greatly – yet graciously – often provoke the same response. They are a spectacle of grace to the rest of us, like flaming bushes unconsumed, causing onlookers to ask, like Moses, "Why is this bush not burned up?"

Mike King is my burning bush.

His strength and stability is evident to all who know him. Although his gentle and quiet nature is housed in a broken body, he keeps his heart bright, and his smile, fresh. Such strength can only be explained by the miracle of God's sustaining grace. Mike King's life is on display, causing others to wonder how it is he is not consumed by his hardships.

The first time I met Mike was on a cool autumn evening back in the 1990s. He came wheeling exuberantly through the kitchen door of the Eastern Pennsylvania farmhouse, late for dinner. He may have been late, but no one – certainly not me – seemed to mind. Everyone welcomed him as warmly as they would the town mayor. Strong and handsome, Mike carried with him a sense of great presence and import. He was obviously admired and well respected by all.

And there's a good reason why. One would think that Mike, at the age of 20 when he lost use of his legs in an accident, would have collapsed in despair. He was strong, virile and vibrant, with a bright future ahead of him. But this bush was made of something quite unique – and to this day, it is this remarkable man's gentleness and good humor, which causes us all to marvel at his faith.

Over the years since the 1990s, Mike King and I have enjoyed serving together in Christ's kingdom. Whether leading sessions at a Joni and Friends' Family Retreat, or counseling disabled American servicemen at one of our *Wounded Warrior Getaways*, or delivering wheelchairs and teaching in China, Mike is a ready partner in the Gospel (he even married Sharyn, a Joni and Friends co-worker). He is so much a part of the fabric of Joni and Friends, our ministry even produced a TV episode on his life!

My point is, Mike King is always willing to go where the kingdom is weak in order to make it strong. He's always on call to take the Good News where the world is bleeding out of control. And I *love* him for that.

The man whose autobiography you hold in your hands may be lacking literal use of legs, but isn't it ironic that God should use a paraplegic to move the rest of us to step out and live life to the fullest? St. Irenaeus wrote centuries ago, "The glory of God is man fully alive." That's my friend, Mike. In a world that is splitting apart at the seams, and filled with anxiety and despair; in a world that is clueless as to how to 'own one's weakness;' in this brutal age of anti-heroes, we need, as never before, the stories of courageous people who know how to live with hardship. People who know how to burn with life-passion, yet not be consumed. You hold in your hands such a story. In this exceptional book, you will discover a man who is very ordinary, yet simply extraordinary. And like me, you will think, *If Mike can overcome his limitations, I can, too.*

People who suffer greater conflicts *always* have something to say to those who suffer lesser ones. *Powered to Move* is *that* gripping; it is *that* important. Just begin flipping a few pages and you'll understand why.

Joni Eareckson Tada
Joni and Friends International Disability Center
Agoura Hills, California

Preface

I grew up in a Christian home where my parents showed me love and discipline throughout my adolescent years. I always had adventure in my blood. As kids, my brothers and I would often venture into the woods with my uncle to build huts and tree houses. We built ramps to see how far we could jump our bicycles and later we graduated to seeing just how far our motorcycles could fly off those homemade hills of fun. That was all before my accident in 1978, but the dauntless disposition remains to this day.

In life, you or someone you love will experience a variety of trials, accidents and challenges. I know being a Christian doesn't spare us from struggles, but it is the most important part of my recovery. My faith took me through the darkness and brought me a deeper understanding of what it means to have a personal relationship with Christ.

I live life with disability, but I live with eternal hope. Everyday of my life I meditate on Romans 5:1-5:

> *Therefore, since we have been justified through faith, we have peace with God through our Lord Jesus Christ, through whom we have gained access by faith into this grace in which we now stand. And we boast in the hope of the glory of God. Not only so, but we also glory in our sufferings, because we know that suffering produces perseverance; perseverance, character; and character, hope. And hope does not put us to shame, because God's love has been poured out into our hearts through the Holy Spirit, who has been given to us.*

I'm not just sharing the story of my life, I'm sharing the promises of faith. In these pages you'll meet the friends who encouraged me, the family who prayed for me and the community that surrounded us in one of the darkest times of our lives.

My life's mission is to reach others who are struggling. The contact information for our organization, Powered to Move is printed in the front of this book.

Let me know how I can help.

"Before I shaped you in the womb, I knew all about you. Before you saw the light of day, I had holy plans for you…"

JEREMIAH 1:5 THE MESSAGE

IMAGINE BEING 20 YEARS OLD, strong and adventurous, with your whole life ahead of you, setting out on a cross-country motorcycle trip with three good friends.

Picture the freedom, feel the wind on your face, visualize the beauty around you—until the moment that changes everything. You slam into a car that pulls out in front of you, you're ejected from your bike and injured so severely no one expects you to live.

Somehow you survive ...

but you're told you'll never walk again.

On a beautiful day in August 1978, one month after turning 20, I went from being a happy-go-lucky adventurous young man to an angry one; from being an athlete to

a wheelchair user.

"Point your kids in the right direction—when they're old they won't be lost."

PROVERBS 22:6 THE MESSAGE

"You've got to understand, he's a King!"

My four brothers and I had a reputation. Raised on a dairy farm in Chester County, Pennsylvania made us a physical, go-get-em bunch. When we weren't on duty in the barn or in the fields, we were having fun. We were farm boys and athletes, using the competitive nature of sports to push each other to excel as well as achieve individual goals. When people in town would make the reference "He's a King," it wasn't just the fact we were moving fast or starting something, it was also the quality of determination and strong will. When we made up our minds to do something, it got done.

Our house was filled with all the activities a father can teach five sons, but it was also filled with song. I remember the signal to come downstairs and open packages at Christmas, or run outside to locate Easter eggs, was always the sound of my parents' voices harmonizing a tune. We were a family of strong traditions and deep-rooted convictions of faith.

Sundays and Wednesdays were spent at Maple Grove Mennonite Church. Both parents were choir members and Sunday School teachers. When I was old enough to follow in their footsteps, I taught summer Bible School, ushered, sang, and was President of the Youth Group. Although I was active at Church, I never felt qualified. I tended to be shy and reserved in front of people, finding my comfort zone in cross-country sports.

I was made to move.

When I wasn't playing basketball, baseball, hitting a puck across the ice in a hockey rink, skiing down a slope or slicing through the lake on water skis, I was thinking of exotic places I wanted to go. Travel had made an impression on me as a child. Although our farm work kept us close to home, my parents prioritized summer reunions with trips to the mountains, as well as an oceanside weekend spent with various branches of our family tree. When I finished my "obligation" to graduate high school, I was off to Europe with two friends. I was ready to take on the world I'd seen as a child at the World's Fair in New York. I was strong in mind, spirit and body.

Three friends and I planned a motorcycle adventure of epic proportions. We would travel from Pennsylvania to the Pacific Ocean by way of Canada. We'd wind down the West Coast and turn towards home through Washington, Idaho, Montana, North Dakota, Minnesota, Michigan, and the Great Lakes states until we hit the familiar countryside we called home.

The wanderlust of the open road called to me like echoes of my parents' voices from the stairs below on Christmas morning.

We left on August 6, 1978.

"You know when I leave and when I get back. I am never out of Your sight..."

PSALM 139:3 THE MESSAGE

"Be sure to tell Mike that he's going to be alright."

We were packed up. Excited, prepared, and ready to experience the sites, sounds and smells of the road only possible from the seat of a motorcycle. The trip was scheduled to last three weeks, so before I left, I needed to say one very important goodbye. Sometimes you just "know" things, and this was one of those times. My mother's father (Papa Zook) was at the hospital in the end stages of colon cancer. I knew it would be the last time I'd see my beloved grandfather alive. He must have known too, as he had me promise to be one of the pallbearers at his funeral. I agreed, but moved the conversation to dreams of the open road, what we hoped to see, the majesty of the mountains, the sun on our faces the wind at our backs and the colors of fall just beginning to show in the leaves.

Greg Petersheim, Merv and Ron Stoltzfus, and I headed out to the West Coast the next morning. We ate when we were hungry, we stopped when we were tired, and we had our eyes open to the beauty that abounded. We'd been on the road for seven days and had made it as far as the Canadian Rockies. Unlike the Colorado end of the mountain range most are familiar with, in Canada, the craggy rocks of the Ten Peaks in Banff National Park erupt from the pines in magnificent authority.

Even in August, the elevation made the trip a chilly one. The off-and-on rain took our body temperature down even further. We'd slept at a youth hostel the night before which at least gave us the chance to put our sleeping bags on a cot instead of the wet ground. By day seven, we were in no hurry to get back on our motorcycles, leaving around 10:00 that morning. The plan was to meet up at the breathtakingly brilliant turquoise Lake Louise.

I was soaked.

By late afternoon the rain finally became a drizzle, but the mist coming up from the road kept my blue jeans saturated. When the sun broke through the clouds, I was ready to take advantage of the scenic lookout to dry off, warm up and take pictures of the abundant mule deer along the banks of the Banff River. The parking lot with its low rock wall, allowed for an amazing 360° alpine view. Close to a hundred people had the same idea I did, that is except for Ron, who was on the road somewhere behind me. Greg and Merv were up ahead, that much closer to the end of our day's journey.

I had warmed up, taken plenty of wildlife shots, and took the last walk of my life, back to my bike. I was headed up the highway to meet my friends, the day was almost over.

None of us would ever make it to Lake Louise.

I didn't see the car pull out in front of me. The police report estimated my speed at forty-five miles an hour. Whether I applied any brakes, I can't say. My last memory of the day is hearing the sound of a horn; too late for me to respond.

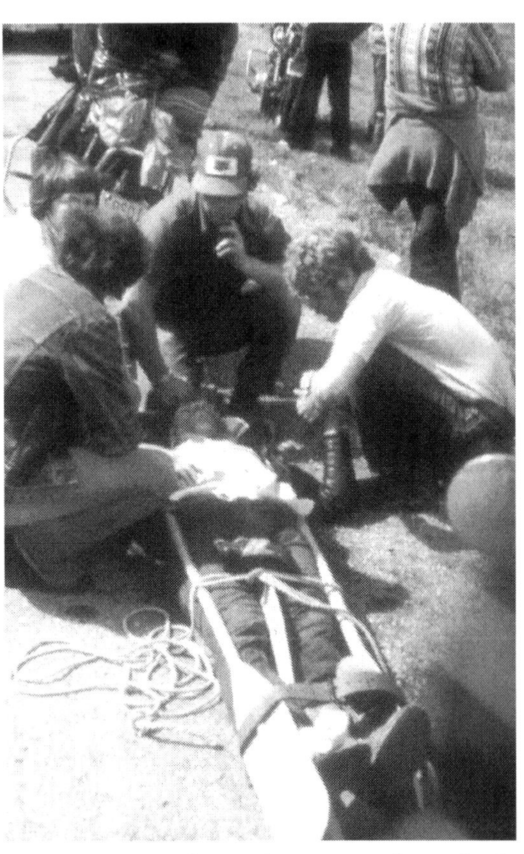

The red lights ahead signaled to Ron something had happened. He was able to weave through the cluster of cars hoping to move past the wreck and on to the lake. As he approached, his worst fear became a reality. He saw I'd been thrown from my motorcycle, and was now lying on the road, with the femurs in both legs broken, massive internal injuries and a severed spinal cord. Greg and Merv had stopped to wait for us but when they saw how bad traffic was backing up, decided to turn around to see where we were in the stagnation of vehicles.

Another accident happened around the same time I was hitting the back of the car and catapulting onto the asphalt—which meant the one ambulance in the area was already in use.

Fortunately for me, a paramedic who'd just come off the river on a canoe trip was caught in the traffic jam, and made his way to the scene of the crash. When he saw my broken legs, he took the canoe oars and used them as splints. He stayed with me until the local police patrol van could take me to Banff Medical Center. The staff realized my injuries were more than they were equipped to handle. An ambulance and medical team were assigned to make the eighty-mile journey with me to the Foothills Hospital in Calgary.

It was 10:00 pm when Greg Petersheim placed the call to my parents back in Pennsylvania. When the phone rings at that time of night (it was midnight in Chester County) it can only mean one thing—there's been an incident or an accident, neither one you want to hear. He didn't know specifics, or that the doctors didn't expect me to live through the night, but he promised to call back as soon as he had more information.

I was still on the operating table.

I spent most of that Sunday night having the internal injuries repaired and the broken bones in my legs set. Seldom is it necessary to do an emergency procedure for a back injury. Discovering the extent of a spinal cord problem, and determining the best treatment for it can be a tedious process I was soon to become intimately familiar with.

By the time I woke up on Monday, roughly 24 hours after the accident, my parents had arrived in Calgary. With tubes in my nose and chest, coupled with the sight of my Mom and Dad entering the Intensive Care Unit, there was no denying I had suffered catastrophic injuries. Fearing the worst, I didn't want to ask questions. The doctors had given my folks and friends instructions not to tell me more than I asked. It wasn't until Tuesday that I turned to my Mom and said, "Why can't I move my legs?"

"You hurt your back."

"... hurt your back." I knew about accidents like that, even without understanding the medical details or having a doctor's explanation, and I knew I didn't want to hear any more.

After a week in ICU, the chest and oxygen tubes from surgery were removed. I was transferred to a west facing room on the ninth floor. On clear days, if I turned my eyes far enough I could see the majestic Canadian mountains in the distance. But the fog of denial, soaked my thoughts as much as the rain saturated my jeans the last day I walked.

I didn't remember crashing; laying on the road or answering the medical staff as they talked to me after the collision. I took each day as it came. The paramedic who attended me at the scene came to the Foothills Hospital while I was still unconscious, and wrote a card introducing himself and wishing me the best. My friends were busy working out the logistics of the end of our adventure; what needed to be done with the motorcycles, who was riding back, who was flying back, what about my cycle? I was banged up, but I was busy believing I could and would walk again.

Ron, Merv and Greg waited until I was moved out of ICU before heading back home. Visitors from the local community, people I didn't even know showed concern. They'd stop by during the day to offer encouraging words of, "Everything is going to be all right," and "Don't worry." I wasn't worried, I was angry. I was frustrated and struggling. It was taking the energy I needed to start walking again, to keep me from shouting at these happy strangers, "Yeah, right. What do you know about any of this!" Along with the unsaid, "This kind of thing can't happen to me!" All those thoughts were bubbling just below the surface of my forced smiles. Depression covered me like an old woolen blanket I couldn't crawl out from under. I was terribly uncomfortable, I hurt, and in the evenings I was alone. There was no majesty to be seen in the darkness. I was flat on my back faced with the mountain of uncertainty.

Was my life worth living if I wasn't walking?

The Foothills Hospital kept me three weeks to stabilize me for transport. The weather was beautiful the day I left. The lower half of my body was numb, but I could still feel the warmth of the sun on my face. I was stable enough to fly, but due to an airline strike, we had to take the twin engine plane of my Dad's friend to Montana. Seats were collapsed on one side of the plane to accommodate the stretcher. My parents and the Foothills' doctor folded in beside me for the short flight to the Great Falls municipal airfield. The only "great" thing was that we were on our way home. It would take two more flights, three more ambulance rides, two sets of six First Class seats and countless people sustaining us, before we'd be in Pennsylvania.

The spinal surgeon (Dr. Ned Schwentker) from Hershey Medical Center and the rehab specialist (Eileen Tymon) from Elizabethtown Rehabilitation were waiting on the runway to assess my condition and assist in getting me off the plane without further injury. I was unstrapped from my three First Class seats by helpful flight attendants, doctors, the therapist and my parents. They transferred me to a gurney and wheeled me into the airport where my four brothers were waiting.

It was the first time in my life I was helpless in front of them. They saw me, laid out on a stretcher, legs in splints, fading bruises, and a broken back. The sight of me didn't "take the 'wind' from their sails" it "knocked the wind" and the words right out of them. There was nothing to say, only a flood of tears to cry.

Finally, I said, "Hey guys, don't cry. I'm home, I'm home!" It was about eleven o'clock in the evening when they put me in my own room at Hershey. It had been a long day. We'd left Calgary at nine that morning.

When I woke up the next morning, Dr. Schwentker, was standing in the room reading my chart. He used medical terms intended to explain the extent of the damage done to my back, but I couldn't comprehend what he was saying. I was still lost in denial about my injury and my future, and I found him to be a cruel guide out of the fog. He looked up from the charts, like a frustrated explorer with a novice traveler as a companion, and asked if I knew what my condition was.

"I know I broke my back."

My memory had been spared the trauma of the accident, but hearing the truth of the tragedy is something I will never forget.

"Yes you did," he said looking me straight in the eyes. "Your spinal cord is severed."

"You
will never
walk
again."

The harshness of his words was as loud in my ears as the blast of the horn I'd heard from the car. My emotions flipped over the handlebars of my optimism, and lay sprawled out on the black asphalt of despair. My hope was now as broken as my legs, and as severed as my spinal cord. My vertebrae had been crushed in the accident, but my spirit had fought the specifics. I turned away. Where was his compassion? None of the doctors in Calgary had ever been so direct or what I perceived from this guy—downright mean! I was enraged, and outraged; angry. I was angry at him for telling me the "facts" in such a fashion. I was mad at the world for the distractions of a driver that stole my ability to be mobile. But most of all, I was angry at God. I was soaked the day I hopped back on my motorcycle, it felt like He was hanging me out to dry. Now dried up and disabled, not knowing what was going to happen, how would I live my life and not be a burden to my family?

What kind of career is there for a cripple?

Later that week my mom came to the hospital and said Papa Zook had passed away. He knew I had been injured and was at the hospital, but was too sick the last months of his life to come and see me. I wasn't able to attend the memorial service, to say goodbye like I had hoped, or to keep the promise I made to him the day before I left on my grand adventure. After the memorial service, my mother sat on the edge of my hospital bed and shared the last days she had spent with her father. She and her sister Anna were with him during his final moments on this earth. As he lay dying, he looked at mom and said, "Be sure to tell Mike that he is going to be alright. He is going to make it through this difficult time in his life. He will overcome because of the strength Jesus Christ gives us."

The last words Papa spoke to his daughter were out of concern for me, her critically injured son. Adapting to life drastically changed would be a challenge and would take the courage those kind of words could instill. The doctor's diagnosis might have pulled me from the fog of denial, but the lifetime forecast of paralysis hit me like a hurricane. All I could see was darkness, and I wasn't so sure I could overcome the storm.

But I never forgot the story.

"...I place before you Life and Death, Blessing and Curse. Choose life..."

Deuteronomy 30:19 The Message

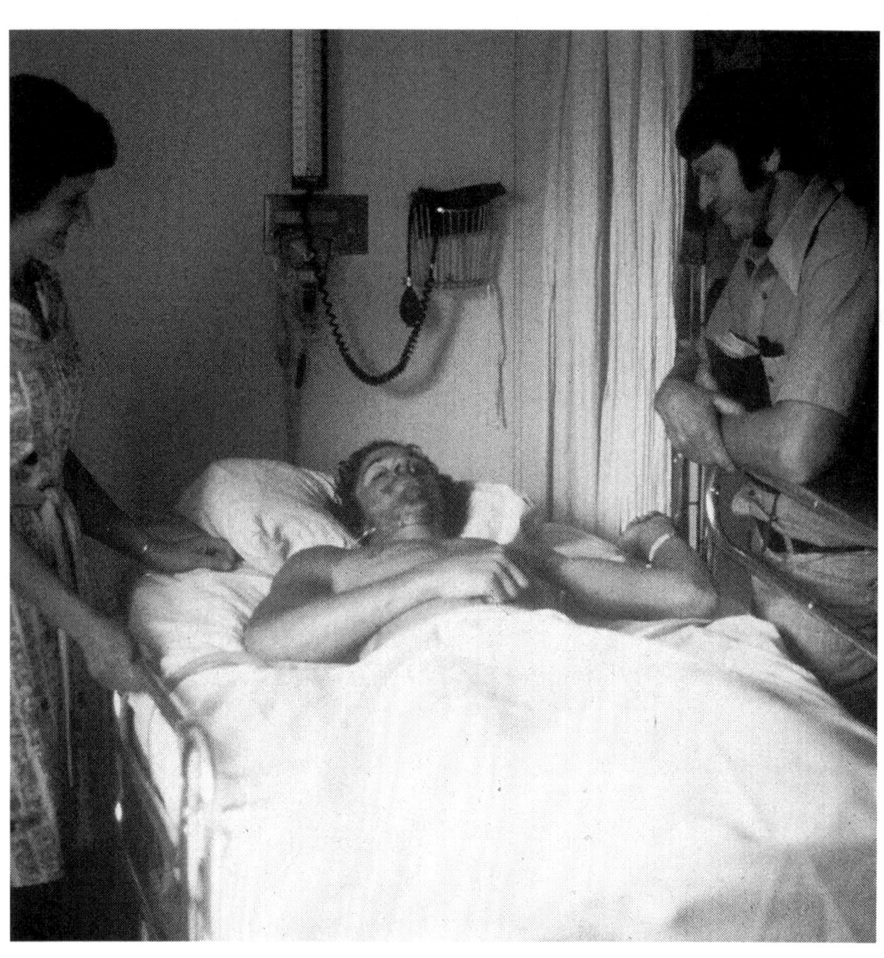

"Nurse, nurse... nurse?"

A hot knife blazed twenty inches down the length of my spine. It followed the path of the surgeon's scalpel, awakening me with the horrible "hello" of hurt. The eight-hour operation was over and I was coming out of anesthesia. The burning sensation down the center of my back was the first time I experienced pain since the accident. The weeks in Calgary, I spent fairly medicated. Waking up the first night with all the tubes in place was just uncomfortable compared to the fire I now felt along the incision; even my shoulders and ribs ached from supporting my weight during surgery. In the recovery room, as attendants tried to rouse me, all I could do was beg, "Please just let me sleep." As soon as the drugs would wear off, I would come to, ask for more medication, and drift back into a state where the reality of my paralysis didn't exist. It was a place where the clock of catastrophe didn't mark the time. Everyday for two weeks, while friends or family visited, the most I could muster was, "Hi," and "Goodbye." But I knew they were there.

Once the incision healed, I was fitted with a body cast that started right under my arms and went to my hips. It protected the six-inch section of my backbone while it fused. I was medically ready to be transferred to the Elizabethtown Rehabilitation Center, but I was not mentally ready. I was without the use of my legs. I was without muscle control below my navel. The upper body strength I'd developed over the years as an athlete, would soon serve me well. I began to push the feelings and thoughts about my "new normal" out of my mind as efficiently as I would be pushing a wheelchair.

I was officially a paraplegic.

E-Town Rehab was an old structure from the mid-forties. It didn't look like a hospital, much less a place of healing. There were no call buttons. Up and down the hallways, the sound of patients yelling, "Nurse, nurse, nurse..." for one thing or another echoed in the unit. It might have been an effective technique for the process of recovery, but it was a drastic change from days of 24-hour attention at the Foothills Hospital and Hershey Medical Center. It took time to come to terms with, and in the meantime depression came for a visit and stayed like a blanket at the foot of the bed. If they couldn't renovate the building how were they going to rehabilitate me?

I lived on the second floor in an olive green room with three guys. Six people (five guys and one girl), who had spinal cord injuries within two weeks of each other would be in the program together. Three of us were paraplegics, three were quadriplegics; it sure beat going through it alone. I adjusted to the environment, the routine of rehab, and the staff.

Eileen Tymon was pretty. She was warm, with a good sense of humor and I was comfortable talking to her. As the head coordinator, she was in charge of rehabilitation programs for patients with spinal cord injuries. She'd been on the tarmac when I arrived back in Pennsylvania, and I knew from that first meeting she was concerned about me as a person. My back was broken, but in so many ways she "had my back" through the long process of recovery. She kept the blanket of depression from working its way up my weakened body.

Staff woke us at 7:00 am. I was given a sponge bath in bed until the hard body cast came off and I was fitted for a removable plastic clamshell jacket. We were served breakfast in our rooms, but my appetite was gone. I forced myself to eat cereal, just to have strength for the exercise routine. At first, I couldn't bend my legs, and my knees didn't extend past a 30° angle. Two aides (Debby Martin and Janet Housel) along with a physical therapist (Betty Husted) worked on my range of motion while I laid in bed. Betty loosened up muscles in my lower extremities, flexing my hip joints and ankles.

I didn't feel a thing.

Once I was able to sit upright in a wheelchair, I spent as little time as possible in my room. Mornings and afternoons were spent in physical therapy, but I'd go to the lounge to play games or watch TV. The six of us (in the program) joked around, encouraged each other and with five of us being guys, it even got competitive. We were like broken brothers, trying to outdo each other in weight-lifting and regaining strength.

Before my accident I weighed 175 pounds, but by the time I got to E-Town, I was down to 155 and was as weak as I looked. I often saw Dr. Schwentker making rounds after he finished his day at Hershey. I came to understand how the "mean" was meant to get his patients to work on recovering from a spinal cord injury, not waste time with worrying about walking. Eileen and Betty told me the faster I learned how to do daily living techniques and complete my physical workouts, the sooner I'd be released. While Betty worked my legs, I lifted weights to strengthen my arms and

shoulders getting the muscle tone back I'd lost during the weeks I laid in the hospital. I worked hard.

Weeks passed, and the range and intensity of my physical activity improved as I was ready. I used parallel bars to stand myself up or do push-ups. I learned to strap myself into the machine that would stand me up by locking my legs and hips into an upright position. It was a good way to relieve the tiredness of sitting so much. I'd sort of jump myself out of my chair over onto the mat where I could stretch out my leg muscles on my own. I started increasing the amount of weights I was lifting.

I perfected putting my pants on.

By October, during the pleasant fall afternoons I would go outside. Nearly every evening there would be a visitor from school, church or a family member. From the time I arrived back in Pennsylvania to the time I was discharged from Rehab (over three months), not a day went by that someone didn't come to visit. On Friday, the 20th I was allowed to go home for a weekend to start adapting to my new life. Leaving the rehab facility, reality set in. It was one thing pushing my wheelchair in hallways designed to accommodate medical equipment, it's another thing to face a house with tiny bathrooms, inadequate doorways

and stairs.

I enjoyed my mother's cooking, but it couldn't compensate for the discomfort. My family home had become a dangerous obstacle course of architecture and emotions. By Sunday I was ready to get back to E-Town. Friends and family were gathered to say goodbye, when the phone rang. One of my best friends, Myron Stoltzfus was on the other end of the line.

"Jon Kent Witmer was just killed."

I was speechless.

Myron didn't know many details, much like the call Greg Petersheim had made to my parents just two months earlier about my motorcycle wreck. Only this phone call contained no unknowns, no hope for getting better, or room to adapt and adjust. Jon Kent died on impact when the gyrocopter he was flying malfunctioned. None of us knew what to say or do. We loaded up and drove out to the Smoketown airport in an effort to get out of the horrible space created by the word "killed," and to get away from the phone that brought the news. I hadn't seen Jon Kent since before I left for Canada. He was one of the few friends that never made it to the hospital or E-Town to visit. We sat in the car unable to approach the scene of the crash and cried.

We drove over to the Witmer's house, and Jon Kent's mother came out. What comfort could we offer other than the camaraderie of tears? We got back to my folks house and started the sixty-mile drive back to Elizabethtown Rehab with muted sobs and silence. About halfway there, I had a bowel accident. Being paralyzed from the waist down prevents the sensation of having to go to the bathroom, and can result in a foul and embarrassing mess. My mother went inside to ask for towels, so my wheelchair wouldn't have to be washed. They got me out of the car, up to my room and cleaned my soiled body and clothes. The staff thought it was the humiliation of my arrival that kept me cloistered in my room, until they saw the headlines the next morning. Their condolences were caring, Jon Kent was my friend and just two months younger than I was. I was supposed to have a wonderful weekend, with family, with friends, and adjusting…

…it ended with excrement.

There I sat, confined to a wheelchair, now broken in more ways than just physical. I was injured in August, my grandfather died in September, and now one of my closest friends was killed in October. The Bible says, "all things work together for the good," but what good could possibly come from this?

What
was
God
Trying
to prove?

Three days later I was released to attend the memorial. After the service his mom and dad sat down with me and shared a letter they'd found at his office. It was one likely never intended to be read by grieving parents, or confused friends. Jon Kent had written a letter to God.

He wrote with honesty, his anger about my accident. My paralysis presented frustration when it didn't get fixed. In his confusion, he made a contract. His agreement with the Almighty: If anything should happen to him, like what happened to me, he wished God would go ahead and take him home to Heaven. He said, "I don't think I can live being paralyzed."

The Witmer's shared the verse found at the close of the letter: "No test or temptation that comes your way is beyond the course of what others have had to face. All you need to remember is that God will never let you down; He'll never let you be pushed past your limit; He'll always be there to help you come through it." (1 CORINTHIANS 10:13 THE MESSAGE)

Jon Kent's death wasn't God making good on His part of the contract. He knew, long before I set out for Canada I'd never walk into my parents house again. He knew the next time I came home, the weekend of October 20, 1978, I'd be carried up the steps. He knew, long before an angry young man grabbed a pen to write about what happened to his friend, the date of his last day on this earth. He knew, the day a grieving daughter would share her father's last words, "Tell Mike he is going to be alright."

He knew, the day grieving parents would share their son's fear that kept him from visiting me in the hospital, and his faith in God's sovereignty.

My friend didn't think he was strong enough to handle life as a paraplegic. I couldn't understand why my life was spared, and Jon Kent's wasn't. Even with the skewed context of the verse, I grabbed the twisted rope of hope and began to hang on. Maybe—God thought I was strong enough. Maybe—Papa Zook was right. I began to read the Word, and with the "belt of truth buckled around my waist," to catch the "crap" of self-pity, I remembered a favorite verse, found in the 30th chapter of Deuteronomy. "I place before you life and death, blessing and curse. Choose life..." God won't choose for us, and He won't always choose to change our circumstance, but if we let Him, He can and

WILL change us. He will provide us a way out, He provides us Himself. He provides HOPE in the midst of despair.

That day I chose life.

"Can't you see I'm black-and-blue, beat up badly in bones and soul? God, how long will it take for You to let up?"

PSALM 6:2-3 THE MESSAGE

"We'll be down to pick you up."

After almost three months at the Elizabethtown Rehabilitation Center, my commitment to do the hard work to get out of there paid off. I had a goal, and I accomplished it sooner than any of the doctors or rehab specialists anticipated. I was proud of the achievement. I'd spent time lifting weights to gain the upper body strength for wheelchair transfers, and fulfilled the requirement of learning how to perform bowel and bladder routines by myself. We take for granted what our digestive system does naturally, until the lower half of the body doesn't function on it's own anymore. I suffered through accidents, like the one I had the day I came back to rehab after Jon Kent was killed, and had plenty more to come. I began to adjust the foods I ate, discovering what I was sensitive to, and avoided those that caused an intestinal reaction. Adjusting was part of the reality of a new normal.

Being able to come home during the holidays created a sense of child-like anticipation. I was waiting to get back to my life. But the hard truth I unwrapped that season: my home was a house of unaccommodating obstacles. It didn't take long to see how unsettling getting me settled at home would be. My brothers became porters of a broken body in a wheelchair up and down the staircase, my dad disappeared behind a veil of denial that his son was permanently disabled, and my mother adapted to the role of babysitting her grown son.

When I left rehab on December 15, 1978 my physical well-being had dramatically improved from when I'd arrived three months earlier, but my emotional condition was as numb as my toes. Once again, I returned to a house that was as awkward to get around as my attitude. The following day was the annual Christmas gathering with my dad's side of the family. I told them to go without me. Christmas at our house had always been filled with laughter, joy and singing. I lay in bed, trapped in my upstairs room.

The "Silent Night" was interrupted by sobs.

Christmas morning there were no carols harmonizing from around the tree to signal it was time for the boys to come down. There was only the boys' effort to get me down the stairs and ready to go to my grandmother's house. It was the first Christmas without Papa Zook, and although there were twelve of us together to celebrate, the losses we all were dealing with were heavier than the snow plows of Pennsylvania could push away.

New Year's Eve was typically spent at a church lock-in supervising the Youth Group. I didn't go. I was already locked in misery and I wasn't sure I could find a key of hope to get out. The change in my world wasn't marked by seconds on a clock ending the year 1978. There was no "Happy New Year." My life would be forever marked by the moment a car pulled out in front of me on that summer's day in August. I was classified a paraplegic, but the blanket of depression that had stayed at the foot of my bed during those first months after the accident, wrapped around me like an immobilizing straight-jacket. I would often go days without even going downstairs.

There are five stages of grief to process traumatic loss. During the first two weeks back at home, I had effectively isolated myself, Stage One. Dr. Schwentker's words, "You will never walk again," propelled me past Stage Three, where the bargaining begins. I slipped into Stages Two and Four (anger and depression) like a skier falling downhill on a slope of despair. There were stairs I couldn't climb, bathrooms I couldn't use, dairy farm duties I couldn't perform leaving my young brothers to carry my share of the chores. I was mad at the car that robbed me of my ability to play basketball, baseball, ice hockey, or walk. If I couldn't do the things where I established my identity, I wouldn't do anything.

I was angry!

Being back in a space that couldn't accommodate a "cripple" amplified feelings that the things that made me "Mike," the athlete, adventurer, big brother, dairy farmer, motorcycle rider, independent man, were sprawled out on the asphalt of a Canadian road. The instantaneous crushing of my vertebrae disintegrated a portion of my spinal cord leaving me permanently disabled, but the slow crushing of my will as I struggled to adapt, took me from "dis" abled to unable to care for myself.

I needed my mother. I needed the praying, healing, and nurturing a mother gives her child.

The alarm clock went off early for my mom. She would come in, wake me up, place disposable pads underneath me, and perform the daily routine I'd learned to do for myself before leaving rehab. The injury paralyzed my lower body, inasmuch as my state of mind incapacitated the rest of me. My mother wiped the hind-end of the one she called "her handsome son," like she did when I was a baby. She wadded up the fecal-soaked pads, disposed of them, cooked breakfast for my younger brothers, got them off to school and came back upstairs to get me dressed. She brought my meals and then took my dishes. At the end of the day, she'd help me undress and get me down on the towel-covered floor to bathe me with a bucket of warm water. My father wouldn't watch or help with the daily routine. He kept from communicating his feelings by walking away, down stairs I couldn't navigate.

Fear was settling in and it was a formidable adversary.

A wheelchair, relatively speaking isn't very big, but the problems posed by the shaped-steel frame can be huge. While I was away, the initial weeks in Calgary after the accident, then the Hershey Hospital for surgery, and the months at E-town Rehab, when my brothers and parents were at the house, there was the dairy farm enterprise. Cows don't milk themselves. The community pitched in with operations, and the church would send people to visit me when my family couldn't get away from the farm. Before my return, no one was worrying about Mike, I was being well taken care of. Now I was home, all they could do was worry, and wonder if they could take care of me well, if at all. I sure wasn't taking care of myself.

Pity wasn't having a party, it was on parade. I was its Grand Marshall on the float of anguish, rolling through the house in a wake of anger and despair. My loss of self-worth, identity, and dignity was taking a toll on the household. Visitors came less and less frequently, but the daily phone calls of my two best friends never stopped, despite my best and worst efforts.

They'd call and say, "Hey Mike, we're going out to get a burger, want to come with us?" "No, that's okay, I'm going to stay in today." Day after day, the phone would ring with an invitation to go here, see someone there, do this thing or that thing. I think they were inventing activities, just to see if they could get me to engage or interact. "No," was always my response. Then one day, the phone call went like this, "Hey Mike, we're going out to get a bite to eat and catch a movie. We'll be down to pick you up."

I chose life after the death of Jon Kent, and they were determined to see me start living. My mother's daily selfless service, my families' consistent sacrifices and my friends' persistence, enabled my heart to move my disabled body to a place of promise. For the first time in a long time I understood, to my family and friends I was still Mike, and they were on their way.

I guess I'd better get ready.

"They brought a paraplegic to Him, carried by four men. When they weren't able to get in because of the crowd, they removed part of the roof and lowered the paraplegic on his stretcher."

MARK 2:4 THE MESSAGE

CHORALEERS

LANCASTER PENNSYLVANIA

"You're still Mike King, and you can still sing."

My friends subjected themselves to months of my unfriendly behavior. They stopped by, and they invited me out. They called, and they never gave up. We prayed in agreement for a physical cure. We attended faith healing services and expected a miracle. But when the meetings came to a close, I was still sitting down, rolling out into the darkness wondering what sin was hidden in my past that kept me from being healed. I thought back to days of my youth when I lied to an employer about breaking a window, I called and confessed my untruthfulness. What did I need to do to be the man God called me to be? I saw that man, as one that could walk.

And I wasn't walking, I was struggling.

I remembered the story of the paralyzed man found in the Gospel accounts of both Mark and Luke. During the time of Christ, the sick, injured and disabled were looked upon as cursed, the condition obvious punishment by God for their sin. Yet in spite of the cultural atmosphere toward physical impairments, there were people who loved him enough to tear the roof off a stranger's house to get help. The paralytic's story—a broken man with good friends, was well illustrated by the people in my life. They showed

Christ's love through their dedication at a time when I felt unworthy and unlovable.

That initial night out at the local diner after the movie, I recognized people genuinely cared. I wasn't a guy in a wheelchair to them. I was Mike King, their friend, a person they knew and liked. Those first months back I felt like a prisoner, captive to the restrictions created by my wheelchair. I couldn't round corners, get through doorways, or navigate stairs. I allowed the things I couldn't do to paralyze me further. Because my chair wouldn't fit into the bathroom, I wouldn't do the bathroom routine. I couldn't get downstairs on my own, so I'd spend days upstairs, having few interactions with people other than my family. But when I finally got around my buddies and old classmates, they held up the mirror of friendship, the one that reflects love, kindness and acceptance for who you are, not what you can or can't do physically. My family, friends, and church exemplified the "Body of Christ," even though my body remained broken. They were the kind of friends that would dig a hole through a roof!

It was empowering.

It was life changing.

It was the beginning of accepting life with a disability.

Before my accident I sang with the *Choraleers*, a local music group compiled of graduates of Lancaster Mennonite High School. I enjoyed the music programs and the social life with other choir members. We were well-known in Christian circles, and as a young single man, I liked the popularity and attention I received from females in the audience. We traveled throughout the United States and Central America performing in schools, churches, and National Parks. Our 1978 season ended in the spring, before I left for Canada. The Director, Arnold Moshier, asked me to consider singing with the group in the fall, never expecting I'd return to Pennsylvania paralyzed.

My walking days were over, and I thought my singing days were too. When I transferred to the rehabilitation center, I sent Arnold a message resigning from the group. After all, they traveled, they couldn't take a guy in a wheelchair. The males in the group were swooned over by the young Latin American women. I couldn't handle going from being popular to pitied.

The day after he received the message, Arnold paid me a visit. He let me know very directly I was not being dismissed from the chorale group because of my disability. He assured me, he and the members of the group would do whatever was needed to accommodate me. "Don't let your wheelchair keep you from doing what God intended you to do. Use your voice, and the gift God gave you. I chose you to be in this group because of your personality and ability to sing. That hasn't changed. You're still Mike King and you can still sing. However, it is your decision and I will accept what you decide."

Two days later, I called Arnold and told him I was willing to try and make it work. During the next two months, while I was still at E-town, Arnold would drive up from Lancaster and take me to his house for rehearsal. It was 170 miles round trip every Thursday night. He wanted to make sure I knew the music and got to know the new kids in the group. He'd never worked with anyone in a wheelchair, but he focused on figuring it out. He was comfortable asking questions about how I was doing, and engaged me in conversation during those first dark and difficult months after I returned home.

It was a winter of discontent and depression, but being part of the chorale group brought back the joy I'd felt prior to my paralysis, offering opportunities to use my gift. It helped restore my self-worth and strengthen my faith. I realized I could serve the Body of Christ (the Church) that had served me so well. I started to see my disability as a chance to share God's love. Spring was in the air and in my attitude. Outside the robin's song could be heard floating through the crisp afternoon breeze. The season was changing, and it was time to sing.

By August of 1979, the *Choraleers* were prepared to take their two-week summer tour. I was ready. The house was being renovated, and I was able to take time off from my work as a draftsman. I was beginning to feel more like "Mike King," and adventure still called my name. I'd found my voice and I knew the music; I just didn't know what traveling in a wheelchair would be like, or what problems I might have. We started in San Francisco, and then drove back through the northwest provinces of Canada and the United States, with performances along the way.

Times went well on the trip in spite of some minor difficulties. I had limitations, but two friends in the group learned to pull me up and down steps whenever we encountered an inaccessible venue. They were fearful at first, but it didn't take long before they had the routine down so well, I could traverse stairs as quickly as someone could walk them. Because the group now included a guy in a wheelchair, the Director made sure to schedule programs in retirement homes, hospitals and rehab centers. I enjoyed talking to individuals with physical impairments. After I left E-town, I rarely encountered the disabled. It was nice not to be the only different one in the room.

On August 13, 1979 I finally made it to Lake Louise.

One year to the day, of my last walk.

It was an accident.

Our arrival to Banff National Park on the anniversary of the event was not intentional. It just happened. By the time we realized where we were and what day it was, there was nothing to be done about it but drive on through. The surrounding silence was occasionally interrupted by hushed whispers of discomfort. Strikingly, the weather conditions were the same as they'd been 365 days before; a chill in the air, and the same sort of rain that had soaked through my jeans. Greg Petersheim wasn't somewhere on the road up ahead waiting for me and Ron to catch up. He was seated beside his permanently seated friend in the van. I asked him to point out exactly where he found me lying on the asphalt that late Sunday afternoon. Traffic and time seemed to come to a standstill.

Highway 1A that runs through the park was shut down. We were a mile away from where I'd hit the back of the car. There was an accident up ahead and traffic was being diverted. We couldn't go past the site. Just a year earlier I had been under a surgeon's knife struggling to survive. In the city where I almost lost my life, I was alive, there to lift my voice in praise to the God who had spared me.

Later that night I heard on the news, six people were involved in the accident we passed.

No one survived.

Greg and I stayed with the Penner family who had hosted my friends while I was in the Intensive Care Unit at the hospital. We exchanged our personal remembrances of events the last August we were together. Greg shared that when I was in the operating room and the staff were saying they didn't know if I would survive, he felt God was telling him I was going to make it, and I was going to walk again. I think it was what we both needed to hear and hope for to move forward.

My physical capabilities changed in Calgary on August 13, 1978. My spiritual possibilities changed there a year later. I began to believe my life had been spared for a purpose, and I decided to let God use me the best way He can.

If it's from a wheelchair,

I'll be rolling on down the road.

"By no means do I count myself an expert in all of this, but I've got my eye on the goal, where God is beckoning us onward—to Jesus. I'm off and running, and I'm not turning back."

PHILIPPIANS 3:12-14 THE MESSAGE

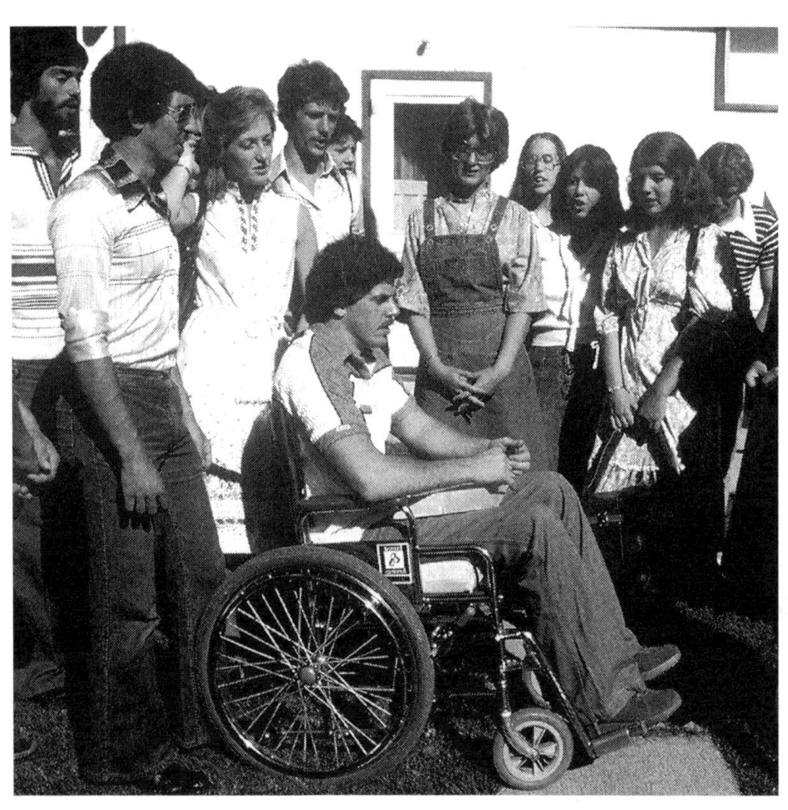

"What are you going to do next?"

When I left on the motorcycle trip, I planned to come back and go into business with my Dad. He'd teach me what I needed to know to take over the farm. I took just enough classes in high school to get by, never thinking about a higher education. The collision changed all that. Now it would take college to access resources, and accomplish the things I wanted to do. My injury challenged me to find a career outside the pastures of Pennsylvania.

I wasn't going to be a dairy farmer.

My summer on the road singing with the *Choraleers* expanded my horizons and broadened my view of the world. I began to understand my friends would be there for me when I needed them. If there were stairs I couldn't climb, or a vehicle I needed help getting into, people stepped up and pitched in. The vulnerability I felt diminished and I started to express my emotions better. While my life had new hurdles, there was fun to be had and songs to be sung.

When I wasn't performing, churches started offering me opportunities to speak, lead weekend retreats with their youth groups, and teach Bible studies. In some ways I served as a good example (overcoming obstacles) and a warning (against dangerous activities) at the same time.

Lauren Martin and I became friends during the '78 Spring Choraleers tour. After the wreck that summer, he visited while I was in rehab and openly expressed he didn't know how he could help but he was willing. He seemed to be around whenever I needed him. He encouraged me to get a degree and volunteered to be my roommate. Hesston College was the first place I'd live away from home since my accident.

I would be their first student confined to a wheelchair.

My freshman year there was no legislation in place for people with disabilities. I hadn't let accessibility of buildings and public places slow me down. I had traveled across the country, even down to Central America. But I had friends, family, and a community committed to helping. When I arrived at Hesston, I became the center of a major debate within the administrative staff. Most of the buildings on campus had their main activities on the first floors, but not all the places I needed to go were accessible. My professors became my advocates. Minor changes were made in my dorm bathroom, curb cuts and ramps were put in, but the more extensive renovations were an issue. I was a problem.

Guilt came knocking on the door of my disability.

The people in a position to make the changes, knew changes needed to be made. I sensed a barrier between us greater than any curb on campus. Some argued if they accommodated a person in a wheelchair, they'd have to offer everything in Braille so a blind student could get along at Hesston. They were the ones blind—blind to the humanity that still resides in people impacted by disability.

The administration stayed at arm's length, never wanting to become emotionally involved with the guy rolling around on their campus. At first students approached Lauren before coming up to me. He'd return to the dorm and say, "This guy was asking me how to talk to you." It seemed kind of funny, I'd been in front of audiences, been applauded and here I was among peers put off by a piece of steel with wheels. If I felt the unease of a classmate, I'd say, "Hey, I'm normal and I'm not mad about my disability." That usually made them comfortable, allowed them to ask questions about my accident, and eventually we all came up with wheelchair jokes.

One day Lauren and I met for lunch as usual. We were ready to take on the ten steps down to the cafeteria. We tackled the challenge daily, but that noon a few steps from the bottom, his foot slipped. The sound of a wheelchair colliding with concrete caught in between two bodies made quite a noise. We fell the rest of the way into the cafeteria, right in front of a major contributor to the College who happened to be eating there that day.

Within a few weeks a wheelchair lift was installed at the entrance.

I joined music groups, I toured, traveled, and studied photography. I gained an education. When I returned to Elizabethtown for my annual checkup, one of the staff members asked if I planned to work at the facility when I finished school. The question was well-timed. I enjoyed my Church Ministry studies at Hesston, but I'd need a degree in social work to be employed by a rehab hospital.

When I finished Hesston, I decided to complete my four-year degree at Tabor College. In January of 1983, I had an opportunity get academic credits with a visit to Brazil where my cousin Kevin was working. He was there on an agricultural production assignment under the Mennonite Central Committee, a worldwide relief and service organization. My back had been broken, but not my spirit of adventure. I invited Lauren to come along.

The first semester at both Hesston and Tabor Colleges were uneasy, but when we arrived in Brazil, it caused more of a calamity than the day we fell through the lunchroom doors. People with disabilities in the villages of Central and South America don't go out in public. They live in an environment that a few curb cuts cannot fix. There is no benefactor that can make their world accessible. Many of the places we went, I had to be piggy-backed in the building up the stairs with my chair folded and carried because the doorways were too narrow to pass through.

We met with Brazilian farmers experimenting with crop irrigation Kevin engineered and visited villages where he was digging wells to supply pure drinking water. We vacationed on the beach, took a cruise and drove to the city of Salvador. Kevin was asked over and over why I was in a wheelchair. I couldn't understand the language, but the look in their eyes was familiar; I had seen it on campus before people took time to get to know me.

I got back from Brazil and was having dinner one night with my parents sharing my experience. My dad casually said, "What are you going to do next?" I'm not sure if it was the shift in his attitude, coming to realize nothing was going to slow me down, or mine, that gave birth to the idea I plainly stated that evening without much consideration.

"I'm going to go across the country
in my wheelchair."

"I've learned by now to be quite content whatever my circumstances. Whatever I have, wherever I am, I can make it through anything in the One who makes me who I am."

PHILIPPIANS 4:13 THE MESSAGE

of a
WHEELCHAIR
MARATHON
Alaska To Washington, DC

"How serious are you about this?"

In the summer of 1978, I became part of the community of people living with a disability. Those first few months I struggled to find purpose and direction for the life I would now be living from a wheelchair. My family, friends, church, and college classmates made it possible for me to redirect my goals and envision new dreams and challenges. They willingly traveled down the emotional road of recovery embarked on out of love. It didn't matter if it was going to a movie or to Mexico, joining the *Choraleers* or off to college, curbs, corners, steps or stairs, I was included and enabled.

When I told my parents I wanted to go across the country in my wheelchair, I didn't know the lower forty-eight states had been crossed by two pioneering wheelchair athletes, George Murray and Phil Carpenter. It wasn't such a crazy thought after all, the crazy part came in when I decided to go farther and start in Alaska! I went back to college and shared my idea with my roommate Doug Peachey. He just laughed and said, "I'll give you a dollar a mile." I was quick to point out, "Do you realize we're talking about 5,600 miles?"

"Doesn't matter, you'll never do it."

I got mad.

My childhood environment had nurtured an athletic mentality. If there was a physical challenge, I could train for it, learn the mechanics of the sport, get into shape and achieve just about anything. Here was my friend saying I "couldn't" do something. Every time I mentioned it, Doug would say, "It's not you, it's just not possible." I wondered if he was right.

Paralympic athletes were making headlines during the wheelchair racing exhibitions at the '84 Olympic Games in Los Angeles. Physical fetes that seemed impossible for those affected by disabilities were inspiring people around the world. It had been over six years since that fateful day in the Canadian Rockies. I'd travelled back to Canada, to Honduras, Brazil, and throughout the Midwest, but I needed a challenge after I graduated from college.

I needed the challenge of a lifetime.

The idea of pushing my chair from Alaska to Washington, D.C., never left my mind. I went home for Thanksgiving and shared with my friend Myron the inspiration that had spun around like the wheels on my chair for almost two years. I had a month left before getting my degree. If during my cross-country trip I could benefit the disabled community and sensitize the able-bodied, I would multiply the impact of my physical accomplishment. The financial initiative offered by my roommate ignited a desire to use the trip to raise money for rehab centers we could visit along the route. I took Myron the plan outlining my thoughts. He had the business experience to pull it off, but he asked for a month to think about it.

My parents grew concerned. When friends and neighbors got wind of the plan, they never spoke to me about it, they sought out my folks. "You need to talk to Mike," was a common refrain. The echoes of agony from my ill-fated motorcycle trip were frightening. They wondered if I was taking on too big of a physical hardship, what if I injured myself further, what if I didn't finish? But they saw my determination. They understood the need I had to prove to myself, to regain a sense of value and purpose and eventually they came around.

"How serious are you about this?" asked Myron at the other end of the phone line.

Convincing him of my commitment wasn't hard, we'd been close friends since high school. Four of us guys (Myron Stoltzfus, Glen Smoker and Jon Kent Witmer) were almost inseparable. We played sports, hunted and hung out, even ditched dates to watch Saturday Night Live on the weekends. The reason Myron wasn't on the trip to Canada in 1978 was he didn't like motorcycles. He liked them even less after my accident. He was the one who made the call when Jon Kent was killed. His sudden tragic death created a void; nothing to be done, no plans to cancel, no dreams to embark on, only a phone call to make. Perhaps helping me complete an epic journey was his way of dealing with the loss we shared and felt so deeply. There was nothing he could do for Jon Kent.

There was a lot he could do for me.

Myron talked with his lawyer, Doug Good, on the most advantageous way to accomplish our plan to fund the trip and raise money for rehab centers. His recommendation resulted in the formation of a non-profit we named *Hope for Life.* We chose a Board of Directors that would give us credibility in the community. We enlisted local businessmen, my pastor, and Eileen Tymon who oversaw my rehab at E-town. When Dr. Schwentker, the Medical Center surgeon who told me I would never walk again joined the Board, my parents were convinced I was physically ready and able to make the trek.

My school friend, Chris Slabaugh, Myron and I visited the local AAA *(Automobile Association of America)*, and told them the places I wanted to travel through. They helped map the route. Rehab centers receiving funds from *Hope for Life* were located in five major cities. AAA suggested Chris make phone calls to learn about road conditions and make adjustments if needed.

Myron researched cross-country trips other wheelchair athletes had completed. Looking at the 1981 journey across the lower forty-eight made by Murray and Carpenter, as well as one in 1983 by John Enright, helped him calculate how many miles I might be able to do in a day. He connected with people who had run coast-to-coast for the Cancer Foundation to learn how they generated interest for their fundraising efforts. They graciously sent literature on how they organized their trip. Help, advice and support were coming in from all corners of the country. It was exciting.

I knew from the beginning I couldn't do this alone. I told Myron I needed a van behind me, traveling with at least two people to protect me from oncoming traffic. As the plans solidified, it was clear I required more than escorts. We needed help to publicize my arrival in towns and cities and to set up fundraising and speaking events. Local media connections should be established to promote the issues of people with disability. There was also food and lodging to be arranged. Myron contacted the local college to see if he could work out a summer intern program for students. They would get four hours of credit for doing work in their field of interest and I wouldn't have to worry about logistical details.

In early February, I started putting in five miles a day and I couldn't believe how out of shape I was. It took me four hours to complete that first five-mile day. I didn't have logistics to worry about, but I worried I'd never make it. The laughter of my roommate haunted me.

Myron and the team had put in hours of effort and research to calculate how many miles a day I would need to cover. The map was plotted with estimations of the numbers. They determined alternate routes where road conditions would not be favorable to a guy pushing a wheelchair. The first day I started training, clocking in at a little over one mile an hour, it would take me three years to get to Washington, D.C.! That was a crazy calculation for my crazy idea. I had trained with weights since my injury to increase upper body strength, but this would take more training than I'd imagined. I needed to build up my endurance and my speed. As time went on I developed a rhythm and my conditioning improved. I got the five miles down to forty-five minutes. I began to add miles and hours building stamina. By the time I was ready to leave for Fairbanks I was up to fifty miles a day.

The Board of *Hope for Life* effectively spread enthusiasm about the trip. In late April, just days before I flew to Fairbanks to start wheeling, some five hundred people gathered in Lancaster County for a send-off dinner and fundraising event. The community and friends that had stood by my family during the early days after my accident, caring for my younger brothers when my parents went to Canada, chipping in with farm duties, remodeling the house to make it accessible, came together again in an overwhelming show of support. I had come a long way since the accident; it seemed in many ways much farther than the challenge that now lay ahead.

The Public Relations team (Steve Engle, Tim Haines, Lisa Wagner and Teri Shimmer) were in advance of us by two weeks. They were driving the route and checking road conditions. Steve would go to the police station or city hall to tell them about our work and inquire about setting up a rally or fundraising dinner. He'd connect with the Lions Club or Jaycees. He'd stop in diners and talk to locals explaining our efforts. The other three built on his foundation, finalizing lodging, press conferences, interviews and visits to rehab centers and hospitals.

We were as prepared as we could be.

April 22, my brother Curt and our cousin James Graybill left in the support van for Fairbanks, Alaska. They would be the first crew to follow me. I flew from Philadelphia on the 26th. We reunited in Fairbanks on Saturday morning, April 27th.

I had a great crew that had put in months of hard work. But in the end, it would be up to me.

I had to push myself

across 5,600 miles of open road.

"From the ends of the earth I call to you, I call as my heart grows faint; Lead me to the rock that is higher than I."

Psalm 61:2 NIV

4

DAY	DATE	DISTANCE TRAVELED	COUNTY	MILES
110	Aug. 16	Youngstown, Ohio - Clintón, Pa.	Allegeny	56
'	17	Clinton - Pelmont	Armstrong	51
3	18	OFF		
114	19	Pelmont - Johnstown	Combria	43
115	20	Johnstown - Water Street	Huntington	58
116	21	Water Street - Mufflintown	Juniata	43
117	22	Mufflintown - Harrisburg	Dauphin	45
118	23	Harrisburg - Gap	Lancaster	54
119	24	OFF		
120	25	Gap, Pa. - Elkton, Maryland	Hartford	51
121	26	Elkton - Baltimore	Baltimore	50
122	27	Baltimore, Maryland - Washington, D.C.		50
				5355 Grand Total Miles

from AAA Trip meter

Phila area

VAN Trip Odometer totaled 5,605.8 After all days were totaled

"Just because you try something and don't finish doesn't mean you've failed."

My friend Don Shenk was living in Fairbanks and met us when we arrived on the 27th. I'd been flying for over 11 hours, my road crew had driven more than 4100 miles, but for some reason, youth or delirium, we thought it would be fun to drive 7 hours down to Anchorage so I could participate in their annual wheelchair race the next day. We forgot to *spring forward* with our clocks and wound up leaving Fairbanks an hour past our schedule. We missed the start of the race but I was determined to do the course anyway. I didn't break any records but I was on the road, and ready to roll.

We'd plotted miles on the map, we scheduled stops for speaking engagements, we enlisted locals for our lodging, but we did not evaluate the effects elevation would have on my physical stamina. We failed to calculate the body's circadian rhythm fighting against perpetual sunshine. When the sun finally shows up in Alaska after months of winter hibernation, it's as if the world stops turning on its axis to welcome the rays. From around 4 am until 10 o'clock at night the light in the sky creates the illusion of a continual day, with shadows ushering in the dawn and shades of night falling long after bedtime.

Don planned a 15 mile race from Fairbanks to North Pole to get local interest and media coverage to kick off the event we aptly named *The Challenge of a Lifetime.* Five wheelchair athletes joined me at the start of the journey. I wasn't thinking about Washington, D.C., I was sizing up the other competitors and strategizing on how to win the race!

It turns out Santa Claus does not live in North Pole, Alaska. If he did, I'm sure he would have greeted us at the Finish Line. I was not the winner, I was not the loser, I came in third.

My 5,600 mile journey had officially begun. The sun was high in the sky, there was three feet of snow on the ground, and I was on the other side of North Pole alone. The fanfare and the racers now behind me, the brutal Alaska Highway stretched out before me.

At mile five, blisters started forming on my hands. By the time we stopped for the evening I was exhausted, but found it hard to sleep. My body was on Pennsylvania time, a 5 hour time difference, and my mind was out on the blacktop of the road. That night Curt and James spent time setting up the chair and making adjustments after seeing how the other wheelchair athletes positioned themselves and their wheels.

At the end of the first day I was 15 miles behind schedule.

As I started the second day, I knew I couldn't keep falling behind. It felt like I had the brakes on. My tires were wearing out. I looked back and could see rubber marks on the road, something wasn't right. Curt and James could see the struggle I was having, not just with the incline of the road or the increasing elevation; they could see the battle I was waging with myself. They'd drive up beside me and ask, "What do you want us to do? Let us push you up some of these hills." I yelled back at my brother, "Are you kidding me! I'm supposed to be pushing the distance, not be pushed." This was the same brother that witnessed my initial months back at home, too broken to bathe myself.

He was worried what not finishing would do to me.

What was wrong with me? What went wrong? I realized we forgot to adjust the toe in and out on the wheel angle. No wonder it was taking so much effort with little results. At the end of the second day I had open blisters on my hands, and the vise grip of failure on my spirit.

I was 35 miles behind.

I started the third day thinking, "I'm not going to make it." I had a raw blister on each hand, right where I hit the push rail. I had a cold, and the near freezing temperatures of the morning were making it worse. James pointed out I hadn't smiled in days. I wasn't sure what I had left to smile about. All my training, all the well-wishers back home, all my courage and confidence weren't going to get me over the mountains that stood like unforgiving monuments to what would be the end of my lifetime challenge. I wheeled a hundred yards, turned my chair sideways toward the shoulder to rest, and tried to figure out how to get out of this trip. The more breaks I took, the more I wanted. Throughout the morning and afternoon I carefully thought out the words I would use to tell Myron that I was done. I crafted excuses for myself, for the equipment, for the conditions of the road. I just can't do what I thought I could. Things had to get better fast or I wouldn't even make it into Canada. Forget going to Washington, D.C. The hills, the road surface and my pitiful endurance were blowing my schedule. My concession speech was interrupted by a man driving from Fairbanks back home to British Columbia. He saw the sign on our van "*Challenge of a Lifetime: Wheelchair Marathon ~*

Fairbanks Alaska to Washington, D.C." He pulled over and talked to Curt and James. I kept going; somehow I had to make it through the day. It turned out he was a Canadian Lions Club member and he offered to take our literature to different towns and communities that were ahead of us to get interest for what we were doing. "That's pretty cool, don't you think?" Curt asked that evening. It was hard to share his excitement.

It was the end of Day Three, and I was 50 miles behind.

I was beat.

The 4th day began with a fight over the taping of my hands. The blisters were festering sores, burning with each push of the wheel. I told Curt how to tape on top of the gloves to offer more protection, but it wasn't working. Fear of failure was fueling the fight. I yelled, and he yelled back. Fortunately the bonds of brotherhood won the battle and we headed out towards Delta Junction— the official start of the Alaska Highway.

Spanning 1,700 hundred miles of treacherous terrain, the Alaska Highway was built during WWII to assist in the defense of the Continental United States after the attack on Pearl Harbor. Though a large portion is paved, there was 200 miles of gravel road I would be rolling across. Every spring, crews repair the damage caused by the long months of ice, snow and below freezing temperatures. They pour oil then dump crushed stone on top relying on cars and trucks to pack down the repairs. The weight of a wheelchair wouldn't help the reconstruction effort. It was going to be a very bumpy ride.

About 5 miles down the road, still north of Delta Junction, I came around a turn and saw a group of kids waiting with their bikes.

All forty juniors and seniors from Delta Junction High had ditched school for the day, excited by what I was doing. They introduced themselves to me and asked if they could ride along. How could I say no? James even said I smiled. Pretty soon, I was pushing and they were pedaling. They'd ask questions like, why was I was doing the trip, what was Pennsylvania like? What will it be like when I arrive in to DC, will President Reagan be there to greet me? Many of the questions I couldn't answer. Just the day before, I was ready to call Myron and give up. I was shocked when Curt pulled up beside us later in the day and said we had 60 miles in and did I want to keep going or quit for the day? The student that coordinated the group made plans for some of the parents to pick them all up around 6:00 pm. We kept going until their transportation back to town arrived. It felt like all three hundred inhabitants of Delta Junction were cheering me on. I thanked them for their hospitality; we said our goodbyes and marked the spot on the road where I stopped. We headed off to find a place to stay.

That evening as I lay trying to fall asleep with the sun still high in the sky, I reflected back on the day. I realized I hadn't entertained one thought of my hands hurting, of being tired, frustrated or discouraged. I remembered days in high school when I was running cross-country in my senior year. My coach shared a devotional the day of our last race. He used Philippians 3:12; the whispering remembrance was like fresh snow blowing from the peaks of the Alaska Mountain Range:

"one thing I do, forgetting what lies behind, I strive forward to what lies ahead, toward the prize for the upward call of God in Christ Jesus."

That's what happened on Day Four, those kids helped me forget the miles I didn't make, that was behind me, the steps of the Capitol in Washington, D.C., were ahead of me!

The next day I knew I was going the distance. I wasn't sure I would be on schedule. But I would finish the trip, even if it took a month longer than planned. The pain, or the terrain weren't going to beat me. A good family friend, Sam Umble said before I left for Alaska, "Just because you try something and don't make it doesn't mean you have failed. As long as you've done the best you can every day you are out there striving for it"

People were praying, and God was definitely watching.

I was ready to "press on."

"Do you see what this means—all these pioneers who blazed the way, all these veterans cheering us on? It means we'd better get on with it. Strip down, start running and never quit!"

Hebrews 12:1 The Message

"How about some moose?"

The countryside was breathtaking, with few cars to interrupt the scenic Alaska Highway. You can imagine the surprise when people come upon a guy in a wheelchair rolling down the road. I would see folks driving toward me with their mouths and eyes wide open, wondering if I was a moose or a mirage. Our publicity machine had a limited audience in rural Alaska, so most everyone we met knew nothing about us. Again and again people would drive by and a little while later circle back to confirm I really was pushing myself out in the middle of the wilderness. Whether or not it was to break their own monotony of the 1500-mile highway or satisfy some curiosity, they were eager to engage us to find out what we were doing. Because the economy depends substantially on visitors, they are friendly and open about their lives.

Trappers and hunters we met told tales of the bush and wildlife encounters; among them a story about tree planters mauled by bears. I saw only one and he took off for the woods faster than I could've ever fled. The fear of not finishing was far greater than any fear I entertained of bears or bobcats, moose or the mountains ahead.

It would take over a month for me to get to Dawson Creek, officially Mile Zero. Semi-trucks making runs up and down the highway were the most common vehicles we encountered. We kept seeing the same drivers over and over. They'd never seen anything like our little entourage and the more we saw them the more questions they had for Curt and James on the CB radio. Naturally they asked what was going on and when we'd see them again they were amazed at how far we had traveled. It was an encouraging thing to hear.

Cable News Network featured a story about the trip and there were a few people that had seen the coverage. Some who heard the news made excursions up the highway to look for us and to wish me luck. In small towns word spread quickly and people spilled out on to the streets to watch and cheer. From time to time, folks were actually looking and waiting for us. Knowing the terrain, the distance, the weather and the road conditions, they were still astonished when my wheelchair would come in to view.

Constant vibrations from a day on the road depleted me physically and mentally. The road surface was never smooth and more abominable than an imaginary snow man. The loose stones that failed to get packed down by passing traffic ended up on the edges, frequently catching my small front wheels. With an average speed on a straightaway of 10 miles an hour, holes surprised me and flying rocks bounced around my torso like corn kernels popping in hot oil. On sections that were particularly bad,

I wore safety sunglasses to protect my eyes from the flying pebbles and debris.

Naturally hills were the toughest; add a little loose gravel and I had a real challenge on my hands to keep from spinning or somersaulting backwards. Where it was steep I had to lean forward to keep the chair from flipping over, but if I misjudged and leaned too far, the back wheels would spin out. I could move uphill at around 5 miles an hour, but the really steep ones took me down to 2 or 3 miles an hour or even less. One mountain was three and a half miles from the base to the top. It took me 4 hours to get over it. On the steeper inclines I was forced to shift my weight further forward to keep from tipping backwards, but it did help my strength and momentum for pushing off the rails.

Determination and grunting got me over the mountains. I would go for half a mile, stop for a minute to catch my breath, drink some water, eat a little to fuel my efforts, and then get back to it.

Coming down slopes was a daredevil's tale of guts and glory. I'd just hang on to the front wheels' steering bar to guide myself. To take the edge off my speed I could touch the back wheels with my hand. I'd crouch down in a tuck position where my chest was lying flat on my knees to help the aerodynamics. It shifted a little more weight to the front wheels, but not enough to tip me forward. The longer and wider wheelbase of the sports chair prevented that.

A trucker clocked me coming down the highest point on the Alaska Highway (a 30-mile downhill run) at 65 miles an hour, my fastest speed. My average downhill pace was between 35 to 40 miles an hour, depending on the grade and wind conditions. For safety, coming down the mountain the van took the front position alerting me of sharp turns, grades or uneven surfaces by two-way radios. Twice coming out of Steamboat Mountain in British Columbia, we thought we'd reached the end of the decline and the van repositioned itself behind me. However, we had only reached a plateau. Suddenly there was a steep slope on a curve and I couldn't hold the chair in my lane. Thank God, there were no cars coming because I could have done nothing to protect myself from oncoming traffic. None of us had been on that stretch of highway before and there was no way we could have calculated either the angles of the curves or the steepness of the road.

On the rare occasion we encountered motorists coming toward me from the opposite direction, they would roll down their windows and say, "Oh, man you're going to have a rough day tomorrow. A lot of hills ahead." Was this supposed to encourage me? Or was it merely the only greeting they could come up with for a guy rolling a near impossible distance on a rural road through the middle of nowhere? I learned not to let it get me down because their assessment was more often than not inaccurate. They simply didn't realize what I could manage and what was hard. In fact, the times I heard an assuring "only a few short hills ahead," were far more difficult because they were so steep.

Each morning starting out, we reset the mileage meter on the van to count the day's miles. It was rewarding for me, but for Curt and James, watching the slow clicking of numbers on a dial was tedious. Twenty miles an hour for a wheelchair can feel like flying, but in a van it seems like crawling. We brought along an old bicycle we named Clyde. In the afternoons, as my stamina started affecting my speed, one of them would hop on junky Clyde to keep me company and break the monotony.

We'd been on the road about two weeks, covered close to 700 miles and stopped in Teslin, a small village in Yukon Territory of less than a hundred people. Much of the community's livelihood relies on traditional hunting, trapping and fishing. The morning we set out from the hotel, a dump truck driver pulled up beside me, honked, and cut a sideways "you must be crazy" glance. Familiar with the gaze, I just leaned forward, put my hands on the rails and started pushing. Out on the road as he made runs back and forth from the job site, we kept running across each other. Finally about noon he came roaring by, stopped in front of me and asked what I was doing. When I told him, he responded with spontaneous warmth and the offer, "How about some moose tonight?" We didn't mind circling back because there was no place to stay further down the road. He took us to his home, cooked us moose steaks, potatoes and some vegetables and let us stay there for the night.

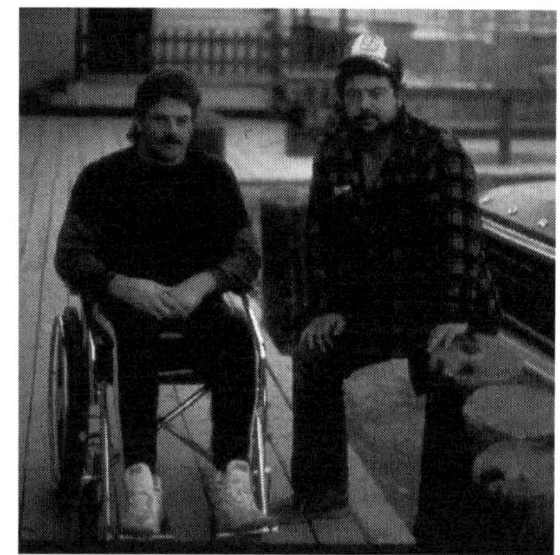

It was an unforgettable evening.

Miles and miles of the Alaska Highway stretched endlessly before me with snow covered mountains urging me ever forward in my quest. There were hills to push up and coast down, as well as interesting towns to stop in, rest and share the purpose of *The Challenge of a Lifetime.* After almost three weeks and 859 miles we came to Watson Lake, in the Yukon. Its notoriety comes from the Sign Post Forest, where tourists have posted over 70,000 of their hometown signs since 1942. We saw people we'd met two weeks and 283 miles earlier in White Horse. They were expecting us, had arranged our lodging, collected contributions, as well as provided for our room and board. There was even an enthusiastic "Welcome" celebration for us later that evening. News was traveling and we were gaining momentum. People were giving money to the cause.

Most everyone we encountered was eager to engage, and it broke the boredom of the open road where townships and villages were few and far between. Often one of the road crew came out and rode the bike with me during the afternoons. Time moved faster and I stopped thinking about how tired I felt when I had someone to talk to. I listened to music, singing along, sometimes practicing the National Anthem, just in case my dream of performing at a Major League game came true. I improved my imitations of cartoon characters and if those passing by would have closed their eyes, well they probably would have been convinced it was Scooby Doo, Donald Duck, Tweety Bird or Porky Pig out there in the Yukon! I was a long way from Sesame Street but my renditions of Bert and Ernie made clever comic cheering companions.

We were coming closer to Dawson Creek and the end of the Alaska Highway, when the fair weather that followed us disappeared. I was drenched from dawn to dusk for two solid days. The summits that had kept me company for 36 days were far behind, slowly transitioning into slopping prairies and small townships as we grew closer to populated areas. I was more than ready for our planned break when Mile Zero was crossed. I needed to recharge, refuel and rest to be ready for events the public relations team were busy arranging. I had a certain comfort level talking to groups having lead Bible studies in the past. But those were delivered after my arrival by car, not coming from pushing a wheelchair down the road, avoiding accidents and nursing blistered hands. There would be no easing into the new routine from road to rostrum. Every night between Edmonton and Calgary I appeared before a crowd of gathered listeners. Rolling up to the podium was oftentimes more difficult than the mountains. I had to remember the purpose at the end of a painful day and communicate the message. Life with a disability doesn't have to diminish your impact on others.

Overcoming obstacles

creates opportunities for influence.

"He will not grow tired or weary, and His understanding no one can fathom. He gives strength to the weary and increases the power of the weak."

ISAIAH 40:28-29 NIV

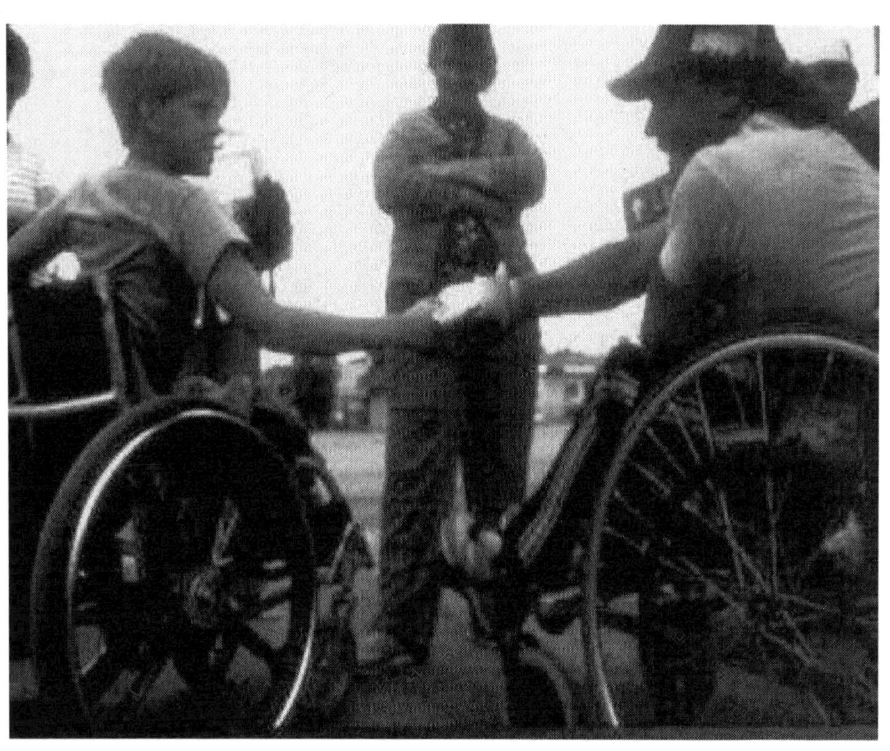

"Hey, I remember you from St. Louis!"

Curt and James flew back to Pennsylvania from Edmonton, and Glenn Stoltzfus and Tim Raber took over the support van duties. Glenn would be with me to the end of the journey. My college roommate Lauren replaced Tim once we reached Denver, Colorado. Originally, we didn't know how important it would be to have the public relations people on the route ahead of us sometimes by as much as two weeks. Even when they wound up being only two days ahead, our ability to connect within communities was invaluable. We learned Mayors, Governors and Major League Ball teams needed lead time to prepare and clear their schedules for us. The road team worked and it paid off.

Meanwhile, Myron was back home in Lancaster doing the accounting with the help of another college student. He worked to manage my speaking engagement schedule and drummed up publicity by phone. One of the difficulties we dealt with was his scheduling me to be somewhere at a time that seemed reasonable sitting in a chair looking at an unfolded map across his desk. Point A to Point B from my perspective involved wind, rain, roadways, honking traffic, as well as interested or infuriated motorists. We had to trust that we were both doing our best from two very different seated positions.

From Fairbanks to Calgary is just over 2,000 miles. I arrived to speak at the Foothills Hospital in Calgary on Day 50. The journey there had been a line drawn on a map, but it was a full circle emotionally. I wanted to see the medical staff and surgeons that saved my life on the operating table, and I wanted them to see me. I visited several patients, including a recently injured physical education teacher. He wondered about rehabilitation and if he could participate in sports. What should he expect for the rest of his life?

They were familiar fears.

The seven years since my accident seemed like seconds as I relived my frustrations in the same hallways where they became crushing companions. I remembered the anger and the despair, my father's guilt and my mother's love, my friends' persistence and my own recent perseverance through the mountains. My words were not platitudes of a passerby; they were anchors of encouragement offered as someone who had survived the storm.

I visited and spoke in nineteen hospitals along the way, concentrating primarily on spinal cord injury centers, but other organizations were included as well. In fact, days I didn't put in any road miles but had multiple speaking and visiting engagements were more exhausting than the days I wheeled sixty miles.

Across the open thinly populated expanses of Montana and Wyoming we'd stop and talk whenever we had the chance. Friendly residents and ranchers took us into their homes, sharing meals and their lives with us.

In Roundup, Montana a young boy who was injured the previous year rode all the way through town with me in his wheelchair. He had no steering capacity, but by holding onto it, I was able to direct the path his wheels would make in tandem with mine. A smile was on his face and the thrill of speed was in his eyes as we went downhill faster than he had ever been able to manage on his own. It's one thing to feel athletically strong, but to have opportunities to feel like a hero are unparalleled.

The schedule was intense and covering the miles was a constant pressure. Mike King needed to show up on time when the governor of Colorado declared, "Mike King Day," as I arrived in Denver! "Mike King Day" indeed, it was the day I spoke to Dan Reeves of the Denver Broncos, one of my childhood heroes.

It was the Mile-High City, but the warmth of the receptions compensated for the effects of the elevation on my ability. Down the road in Colorado Springs, the wheelchair basketball team rode through the city with me.

We stopped at the Craig Rehab Center where over a hundred patients and staff came to hear me speak in the gym. The area had recreation facilities available for wheelchair users with access to modern equipment, as well as accessible camping and rafting trips. They were a healthy group, knowledgeable about

paraplegic's abilities. "Spalding Hospital Welcomes King of the Road," greeted us at the next stop along with animated cheers of the crowd gathered for the fundraiser.

The weather was pleasant through the Rocky Mountains, but as we entered the Great Plains states of Kansas and Missouri the July temperatures climbed up over 100°. We came into one small Kansas town and a little girl and her grandmother were waiting for me. "Why in the world would you ever want to do anything like this, especially at this time of year?" It was 104° that afternoon and I knew she questioned sincerely. I told her about raising money for organizations, visiting hospitals and sharing with different groups. After hearing the explanation she said, "Boy, I'd rather be swimming!"

The sweltering days of summer created the illusion of watery oases on the asphalt, I was thinking of swimming not pushing the wheels around and around and around. The heat of those days had me going through five gallons of water. I would drink three and pour two over me to control my body temperature. It was a fight to stay hydrated, motivated and moving on down the road. I was running behind schedule one day trying to make it through Emporia, Kansas. I'd just had a record day of 80 miles from Dodge City to Wichita, but the oppressive heat and constant sweat dampened my spirits. Seven miles out of town, campus police from the State University came up beside the van.

Was this day about to go from bad to worse?

Lauren and Glenn pulled over to see what they needed. I stopped as well wondering what was up. They were asking if we would come back to meet kids at the university participating in local athletic camps. I worried about how late I'd have to be on the road that night if we backtracked and spent time in town. "Who are these kids?" I asked, struggling not to show my irritation at the inconvenience.

"Six hundred cheerleaders," he responded.

"I'll follow you!" I said, as I whipped my chair around and loaded up into the van faster than any downhill incline had ever impacted my speed.

The basketball and cheerleading camps for the local high school kids were held the week I was scheduled to come through town. They'd heard about *The Challenge of a Lifetime* and asked their coaches if they could invite me to campus. When they realized I'd been there and gone they sent the Campus Police to chase us down on the road. When I had gone through the town, it seemed to be empty, but not all that unusual in the rural communities I was traveling through. When we came back we were surrounded by a thousand people, all there to see me. The six hundred cheerleaders had prepared special cheers that morning for the anticipated arrival. The four hundred basketball guys and girls came out chanting phrases they were taught to keep their spirits up during the physical exercises they endured for training.

"Yes, I can. Yes, I can, Yes, I can, Yes, I can."

They gave me a T-Shirt, stickers printed with the slogan of the week, and a well-timed indelible memory of support and enthusiasm for the road ahead. We drove back to the place marked on the road where my faltering spirit found strength. I pushed on in silence but with the echo of the chant fueling the wheel turns for many miles ahead.

"Yes, I can."

Myron and the road team incentivized me with opportunities to drop in on Major League ball clubs. Farm boys growing up in rural Pennsylvania idolize professional athletes in all sports, imagining eight-foot tall giants to match their renowned accomplishments. In Kansas City, famed baseball player Willie Wilson took us down to the Royals club house and introduced us to a number of the players; among them, George Brett another one of my heroes. We joked around, had a good time and created unforgettable moments.

I was definitely feeling like royalty. A parade had been organized a few miles from my next speaking engagement. Our *Challenge of a Lifetime* van lead the way with two members of the local running club behind me carrying the banner, "Bethany Rehab Center Welcomes Mike King." As part of the parade, several patients were pulled in a horse drawn carriage. When we arrived over two hundred people were at the hospital along with basketball and racing wheelchair athletes. The Mayor and other city dignitaries welcomed us and listened as I shared the goals of our trip as well as issues faced by people with a disability. I went in the facility to visit patients who couldn't be taken outside. There was another reception and a round of "Happy Birthday to You," complete with a cake to celebrate my twenty-seventh birthday and the end of a great day.

The Cardinals played the Philadelphia Phillies the night we were in St. Louis. Later, in the Cardinals' locker room, Tommy Herr, whose home in Eastern Pennsylvania is near mine introduced us to baseball players Darryl Porter, Ozzie Smith, and Whitey Herzog. They were engaging and interested in what I was doing. It was fun to meet Tommy and his teammates. Later back at the hotel I was introduced to Von Hayes, the Phillies's center fielder. We talked a while and I explained *The Challenge of a Lifetime.* By chance, I would see him again when I got into Philadelphia.

He came up to me and said, "Hey, I remember you from St. Louis. Did it really take you only three weeks to get here?"

It was an affirmation I could never have anticipated from these all-star meetings. What was meant as a way to get me through the long and arduous journey served more as validation.

I was an athlete among athletes.

"Sing to the Lord a new song, His praise from the end of the earth, you who go down to the sea, and all that fills it, the coastlands and their inhabitants."

ISAIAH 42:10 NIV

SPECIAL PHILLIES PRESENTATION
FROM PHILS JOHN FELSKE TO
MICHAEL KING IN RECOGNITION
OF HIS CHALLENGE OF A
LIFETIME TOUR

"Oh, say does that star-spangled banner yet wave, o'er the land of the free and the home of the brave?"

Whenever I'd speak in a church, engaging enthusiastic crowds inspired me to deliver a compelling message. I'd bring my racer in so the audience could see how I traveled out on the road. Kids in attendance would play around and ride in it. If they were five or under they'd come up, feel the wheels, grab hold and push it around to see how it moves. Often I'd be sitting, talking to a group of adults and I'd feel myself rocking around and rolling a bit. I'd look down to see a child checking out the chair and examining the wheels. I never scolded or sent them away. I wanted to remove the apprehension of approaching someone in a wheelchair, and the stigma of its steel.

People told me I was easy to talk to. When I spoke in schools, kids approached me without hesitation, unlike my experience as the only wheelchair user at Hesston College. I learned to listen, as there would be no easy escape once surrounded by eager students. I was their cornered captive, but I hoped it would teach them not to fear those who were different when they met people with disabilities.

The details of my appearances were handled by the road crew. They would check to see if it was possible for me to be "Here" by a certain time, and then "There" two hours later. I depended on them to tell me what was coming up as far as road conditions so I could make a fairly accurate assessment of my travel time. Most places scheduled for appearances were directly on our itinerary. If we had a program that was not on the route, we just loaded in the van, marked the spot on the road with chalk and drove to the destination. Afterwards, we'd come back, I'd transfer out of the comfort of a moving vehicle and back to the seat of solitude to start wheeling again.

When I didn't have an evening presentation, I tried to relax. About half the nights we stayed in homes and the rest of the time in hotels. I'd watch TV and unwind, visit a little with the host family or go out to a movie. I tried to get to bed by 10 o'clock. During the hottest parts of the summer we were rolling by 6 am to beat the heat.

Mornings passed quickly. I was fresh and raring to go and usually banged out 25 to 30 miles before lunch. But the distance between 30 and 40 miles seemed to take forever. I found that I tired more quickly when we were in the middle of nowhere without people around. I didn't mind being alone, in fact there were days when I wished for a little more privacy without the pressure of having to speak to people riding with me and push at the same time. But I caught my second wind hearing support from the sidelines. I'd knock off the last 10, 15 or 20 miles in no time.

The difficult days were those when I didn't feel well physically. Sometimes I got behind in sleep or I was worn out by the demands I was making on my body and spirit. My hands were swollen most of the summer, mainly the knuckles on my thumbs and index fingers, and there was an ongoing battle with blisters. I treated the sore spots with salve and someone helped me tape my fingers every morning before I put gloves on to protect my skin and keep my hands dry.

I worked hard, ate lots of food, and put away barrels of water to replenish my body fluids. I saw the direct relationship between eating the right kind of food and sustaining my strength to get through the day. Many of the churches generously fed us, but Sloppy Joes and hamburgers lack the nutritional value I needed to maintain my energy for the marathon or more of miles I rolled every day. I concentrated on protein, carbohydrates or foods high in calories. Potatoes, pasta, and pizza became staples for fueling my body's engine. I can't say my day began with the *Breakfast of Champions,* but several bowls of cereal kick-started the morning. We'd stop for fifteen to twenty minutes for lunch, and take a short ten-minute break later in the afternoon. I maintained my stamina throughout the day with trail bars and fruit for snacks.

Up hills, as I slowed in speed and strength, the guys would come out, run alongside me and feed me a banana or an orange. They didn't want to interrupt my momentum so they'd reach over, aim for my mouth and I'd take a bite. If I was going faster than they could pace me on foot, Lauren would ride up beside me on the bike. Sometimes the edibles wound up being smashed on my face instead of winding up in my mouth. But during the longest slope, a thirty-nine mile incline, it took me nine hours and a lot of banana smearing to get to the top.

While going through more heavily populated areas, we usually had a police escort in the lead. I followed, then bike riders and others who joined me, with the van behind. Along the way there were a few negative incidents. The irritation of drivers centered around our holding up traffic for one reason or another. In Garden City, Kansas and a few times in Missouri, we came to a section of highway under construction. My navigation through lanes already narrowed by work crews created longer backups. When the closed lane opened up, occasionally a driver would yell, "Get off the road!" If only they knew how badly I wanted to.

We reached the Pennsylvania State Line after a hundred and ten days on the road and over 5000 miles. We stopped, whooped, hollered and screamed at each other, then dutifully got back to business. It was August 16th, the sun was high in the sky and the humidity was horrible. The Tuscarora Range of mountains ahead were some of the steepest inclines since I'd left Alaska. We had less than two weeks to go but we were in home country.

The road crew slowly navigated the familiar city streets and highways. Our *Challenge of a Lifetime* van drove with warning lights flashing between 20 to 30 feet behind, keeping me protected from approaching traffic. For the majority of the past three months we saw few cars traveling through rural towns and the occasional city. After they passed by, I often noticed people turning to look back trying to figure out what this road show was about. I'd watch as they drifted into the opposite lane and oncoming traffic. They'd hear a horn, and quickly swerve back into the right lane.

Every time it happened, the blast of warning made all the muscles in my upper body tense up. I'd thank God their reflexes were quick enough to avoid an accident.

The day we left Johnstown, Pennsylvania, we were coming down off a mountain onto a highway that widened from two to four lanes. The traffic backed up behind us started coming around to pass. Because of the gradient the van was within 10 feet of me and the two accompanying bikers. We were in the far right lane when a guy came up on us, unaware of how slowly we were moving. Suddenly, he realized he was right on top of us. He slammed on the brakes, but still rear-ended the van. Glenn saw the car approaching and was able to turn off the road onto the shoulder at the time of impact; otherwise it would have run us over.

The driver was pretty shaken, and his vehicle sustained significant damage while our van had only minor scrapes. The twenty-foot long skid marks left behind were evidence of just how close we came to a bad end of a very long day.

Once we were in familiar territory, the traffic increased and so did the fanfare. Locals often lined the streets to watch the entourage of pedestrians, bikes, runners and me, the shirtless suntanned, hometown hero in a wheelchair rolling by. News teams and journalists were reporting the progress nightly. I often stayed after speaking engagements to answer their questions.

August 22nd, a little over seven years from the date of my accident I wheeled into Hershey Medical Center fueled by adrenalin, intent on not being late. My family and friends were there to celebrate the final days of the trip, but also my recovery which started here, in the stark and sterile hallways. Our next stop was the Elizabethtown Rehab Center. It was an emotional gathering with people who had encouraged me back to life.

The next day, runners and a stream of bicyclists that included many of my friends were with us as we made our way to Lancaster.

Hundreds of people were walking or jogging alongside me. I waved to the crowds with one hand, while fighting to hold on to my emotions. As we neared my elementary school, the reception overwhelmed me. Over two thousand people were waiting for my arrival at the West Fallowfield Christian School. Chickens were on the barbecue, the local Congressman was at the podium, and I was regaled as royalty.

We had all come a long way—not measured by mile markers on highways.

I slept in my own bed that night for the first time in over four months. I was exhausted. The next morning was Sunday, and I addressed the congregation of Maple Grove Mennonite Church. Those gathered in the sanctuary had been there for my family in ways too numerous to count. They showed up when my mother and father had to travel to Canada after my accident. They banded together and worked the dairy farm, took care of my younger brothers, brought food when I came home from rehab, and they never stopped praying. This was the community of the faithful that poured the foundation for my perseverance. In my years at Sunday School and services, youth camps and choir I learned, "*I can do all things through Christ who strengthens me.*" During *The Challenge of a Lifetime* I lived it!

That afternoon we went to Grandma Zook's. We sat around the family table laughing, and sharing stories of the road over a home-cooked meal. I felt the pleasure and the presence of my beloved Papa Zook who said, what seemed like a lifetime ago,

"Tell Mike he's going to be alright."

I was at home, I was happy, and I was fueled by the support of my community. With only three more days to finish the trip, that night I went out and pushed twenty miles, propelled by love and in the company of friends and family.

I had a hectic schedule Monday. I spoke at the Hospital in Bryn Mawr as well as the DuPont Children's Hospital. Afterwards, Nick DuPont, one of our *Hope for Life* Board members, asked if he would be hearing me sing the National Anthem that night at the Phillies' game. Early on, Myron had been trying to arrange for me to sing at one of the ball games we attended along the way. The days leading up to our arrival in Kansas City and St Louis, I'd be pushing down the road belting out "Oh, say can you see…" making sure I had the lyrics memorized and I could hit the high note. He would line it up with all the appropriate people and then at the last minute, they wouldn't take a chance on guy in wheelchair messing up the opening of the game. When I told Nick what my experience had been with last minute cancellations, he said, "Wait here." He disappeared down a hallway, and returned with a grin across his face. "I'll see you at the game, and I'll hear you too."

That night, I was less than a hundred miles away from the end of the journey. The comparatively short distance I rolled from the interior of Veterans Stadium to face the crowd of over 20,000 seemed to take the longest time. I stopped near the pitcher's mound. They handed me the microphone and I sang.

"Oh say can you see, by the dawn's early light,

What so proudly we hailed at the twilight's last gleaming..."

The flickering light of a war zone illuminated the flag of our young nation and inspired Francis Scott Key to write *The Star-Spangled Banner.* For seven years I had been fighting a different kind of war, struggling to take back the territory of identity stolen by the enemy known as paraplegia. In the bleachers, thousands of eyes were glistening with tears; some of the spectators knew the distance I had traveled and some heard for the first time that evening during my introduction. Here was my *proof through the night,* I had a flag of purpose to champion the cause of those living with a disability. There were plenty of ramps, but no ramparts, and they definitely were watching.

I got through the song as effortlessly as if I were alone singing in the shower; my dream come true. I was on the field, shaking hands with the players at home plate and pinching myself to make sure I was awake. During the following ceremony, the Phillies' manager presented me with an award recognizing my efforts for the disabled community. It was one of the highlights of the trip.

Lancaster isn't far from Washington, which made it nice to sleep in our own beds the last two days. We marked where I stopped pushing, and the next morning we'd drive back and I'd hit the wheels again accompanied through the congested cities with a police escort. There was a celebratory and electric atmosphere as the motorcade accompanied us down the streets of Washington, D.C. We took the opportunity to stop and interact with the crowds; Eileen Tyman's sister was playing *Born in the U.S.A* on the kazoo in the background. There were hugs and hands shakes and I was even asked for my autograph.

On Wednesday, August 28th, I rolled up to the steps of the Capitol Building in Washington, D.C.

We were welcomed by the House Representative who acted as the advocate for the disabled, along with city officials and various members of Congress. But the faces in the crowd I remember were not of the famous. As I looked out at the hundreds gathered I saw those who had kept the hope: the road crew, my faithful friends, Dr. Schwentker, Eileen Tyman, nurses and therapists from several hospitals, aunts, uncles, cousins, all my brothers, and my Mom and Dad.

After the ceremony and press meeting, my family and I were given a private tour of the White House where I was able to use the President's special elevator. It was installed by Franklin Delano Roosevelt to accommodate his wheelchair.

I'd been on the road one hundred and twenty days.

The longest distance I accomplished in a day was 80 miles from Dodge City into Wichita, Kansas

The fastest speed I attained was 60 mph coming off the highest peak outside of Edmonton, Canada

The slowest was 3 mph when it took me nine hours to make it up a 39 mile slope

I replaced 14 tires on my wheelchair; 9 of those were worn out on the first 1,488 miles of brutal road top on the Alaska Highway

I spoke on 40 separate occasions including 19 hospitals to over 5,000 people

I sang the National Anthem in Veterans Stadium in front of 20,000 spectators

I am the only wheelchair user to receive a speeding ticket in Roundup, Montana for going 10 miles over the posted speed limit of 25 miles per hour (the officer said, "Keep it for a souvenir")

I wore out 14 pair of leather gloves

It seemed like a lifetime since I started the Challenge in Fairbanks, Alaska.

I had pushed myself

for a total of 5,605.8 miles.

"...we know that suffering produces perseverance; perseverance character and character hope."

ROMANS 5:3-4 NIV

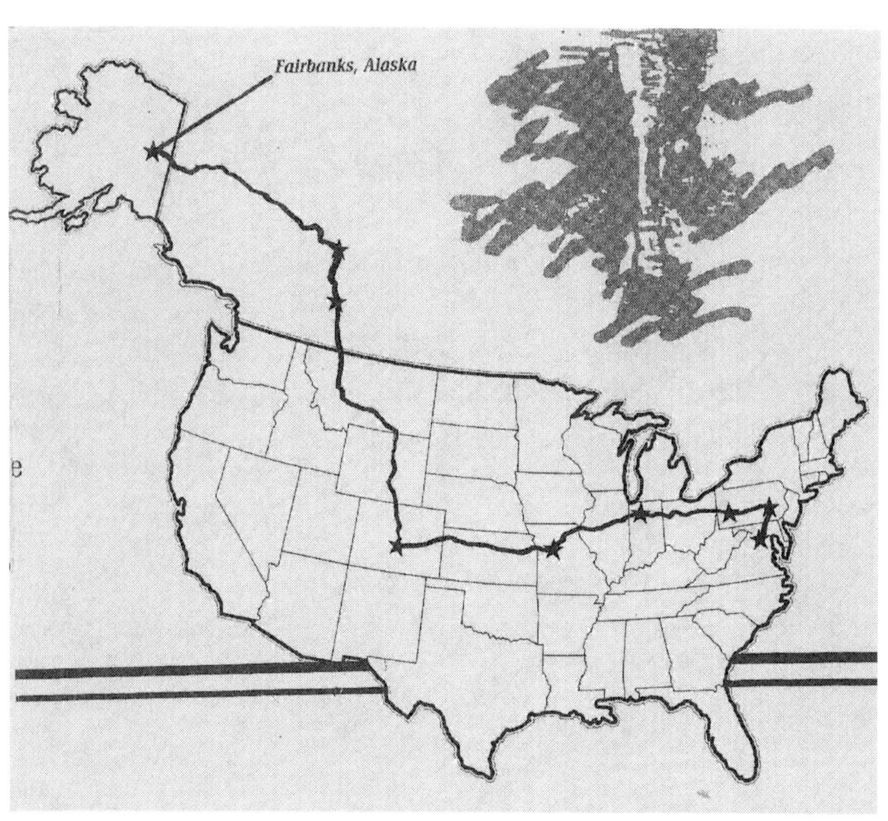
Fairbanks, Alaska

"When they see me introduced as an athlete, they can dream."

I finished the *Challenge of a Lifetime* during the last week of the summer. We spent Wednesday night in Washington, D.C., and headed home to Lancaster the next morning. It was quiet in the car. For the first time in over four months, I wasn't wheeling myself down the road. People weren't cheering me on to the next mile or milestone on the journey. Labor Day weekend, I drove my girlfriend back to Indiana. She was with me the latter portion of the trip and came to realize she couldn't handle what life would be like loving a person with a disability. We said our goodbyes and I drove back to Pennsylvania. It was a comparatively short trip in distance, but it felt farther than the 5,605.8 miles I had pushed.

I was relieved to have the distraction of starting my Fall Semester at the University of Pennsylvania. My plan was to finish my Master's Degree in Social Work. I attended class three days, and the other two I was an intern at a facility for troubled teens. Because I was close enough to the campus, I lived at home.

I was the local dairy farm boy who did something extraordinary, and people love a hero. My parents, brothers, extended family and friends lost a piece of their identity in the shadow of my limelight. If they were around town and being introduced, names were seldom used. They were "Mike King's parents, Mike King's brothers or Mike King's family." When I first started college at Hesston, people would approach my roommate to see how to come up and talk to "the guy in the wheelchair." After the *Challenge,* people sought access to the hometown personality by approaching my friends with, "Hey, aren't you a buddy of Mike King?"

I was a preferred and popular spokesperson for businesses, school programs, and churches. I had a platform to address issues I was passionate about. I used it to educate the able-bodied community on ways they can integrate the disabled with dignity as well as help them regain normalcy after an accident. A lesson from the road that served me well was the importance of paying attention to audiences and individuals. When I was the one behind the podium, sure, people listened. But during the *Challenge* when opportunities to meet professional athletes came up and I was just some guy in a wheelchair to them, I saw how easy it was to discount those around you, especially the disabled. I was determined I'd never treat others the way some of the rich and famous had treated me. I had no intention of going from being one of *those* guys—in a wheelchair; to one of "those" guys—too good to talk to people.

Most Saturday nights, Sunday mornings and Sunday nights were filled with speaking engagements my mother helped schedule while I was in class. I talked about the difficulties of the road, of life with a disability and a testimony of the faith that got me through. I spoke about the journey back to physical health as well as the spiritual healing I experienced. Often, when someone's family member or friend, or even friend of a friend was injured, I was the local go-to-guy called on for encouragement.

"Look what Mike King has done even though..."

I *had* made it. But the role of constant consoler made me uncomfortable.

I knew all the family, the friends, and the faith it took to get me through those horrible first months after my injury. Whenever I went to a hospital room, or rehab facility to speak to a stranger, I wondered, "What if they don't have the support system? What if they don't have family? What if they don't have a foundation of faith to fall on?"

I had been approached by a publishing company to write my story before I even finished the *Challenge.* I prayed the book would share encouragement, hope and faith on a larger scale than I could ever accomplish in a few post-injury visits.

By the spring of 1986 my enthusiasm for Graduate School was waning. Plans were being made to convert the dairy farm into a golf course and I had speaking events scheduled every weekend. Changes at home and in the world of wheelchair sports were taking place and I wanted to be a part of the change, not burying my head in books and studies I'd lost the heart for. My grades began to reflect my lack of commitment. I started working at McGhee Rehab where some of the physical therapists were coaches for the local wheelchair track team. As soon as word got out about the *Challenge of a Lifetime,* I was quickly recruited to join them.

My college years gave me a sense of independence from my family. The wheelchair trip instilled a semblance that with hard work and determination nothing was impossible. Racing with other athletes helped equalize my environment. I wasn't the only guy in a chair. I was part of a team of guys in chairs. We traveled to races to face off against other teams of guys in chairs. We each had physical challenges, but the bottom line, we were men, and we were competitive. I thought with my level of proven physical endurance I'd do okay. After the first race I knew the trip wasn't going to make me a good competitor, I needed to train if I was going to win.

George Murray, the athlete that crossed the lower 48 states in his wheelchair was interviewed by People Magazine before competing in the 1980 Boston Marathon. He told the reporter, "Handicapped youngsters get visited by professional athletes and they're flattered. But they can't go to bed dreaming they're going to be a linebacker. When they see me introduced as an athlete they can dream." That summer, during the Pennsylvania Special Olympics I was able to teach kids in wheelchairs how to become more mobile and active in sports, and I knew just what he meant. Life was full of opportunities. I took advantage of my celebrity to bring a change of attitude in the community towards people affected with a disability.

I spent the summer working at the farm, training and racing. In the morning I'd climb on my brother's back so he could lift me into the Steiger Tractor equipped with two 30-yard haulers. It was exciting to help turn our dairy farm into a golf course. It was clear to me I wasn't going back to school come September. I was home, where I needed to be. I felt useful, productive and empowered.

Since my accident, every winter, I would tag along with my friends during the annual ski excursions. I'd sit back at the lodge, wondering why I bothered to come, sip hot chocolate and stir up resentment for what I was missing. When disability skiing came to the East Coast in 1986, the CEO of the Hiram G Andrews Center invited me on a trip. Don Rullman had long been a fixture in the disability community, championing the cause and increasing adaptive sports activities. From the minute I hit the slopes, to the last run of the day, covered with snow and cold, I was in heaven. Skiing is the one sport that felt the same to my body as it did before the accident, and it definitely showed on my face. When my brother saw me flying down the slope he said it was the first time in 8 years he saw the same smile I had the day I left for Canada.

The Grand Opening of the Moccasin Run Golf Club was in April of 1988. The construction had taken right at two years and it was worth it. My work as the General Manager allowed me the flexibility to train and race almost every weekend. My efforts qualified me for the USA Track & Field Developmental Team for the 1988 Paralympics. I was ready in case one of the other athletes had to drop out of the competition at the last minute. The preparation for racing, time out on the track and in the gym finally paid off in October of 1989 when I participated in the Oita, Japan Wheelchair Marathon. It was the first international racing event in the world held solely for wheelchair athletes and remains the largest wheelchair marathon event.

A few weeks before the race, my cousin Galen came for dinner. I was helping him out with photos of a rig he was selling in preparation for an upcoming trip. He said, "I'm going to Africa." I said, "I'm going to Japan." Then we both said simultaneously, "Take me along!"

My traveling days were far from over. I would have never dreamed of crossing both oceans, visiting five countries and three continents in less than two months; Japan, for the race in October, then we'd leave for Africa the day after Thanksgiving to visit Ethiopia, Kenya, and Egypt. Our flight routed us through The Netherlands, so we figured we might as well see Amsterdam and the countryside while we were there. I achieved my goal in Oita with a finish fast enough to qualify me for the Boston Marathon. The excitement of the adventure practically overshadowed the athletic accomplishment.

Galen's sister and brother-in-law were missionaries in Addis Ababa, Ethiopia. We had problems with our in-country visas and were delayed for a few days. To pass the time, we'd head to the nearby park and sit outside playing chess and attracting a good bit of attention. From my days during the *Challenge,* I was used to drawing a crowd of children. But the African kids were just as curious about the color of my hair and skin as they were about my wheelchair.

With all our paperwork in place we traveled to areas of ministry that were hardly accessible to cars, much less wheelchairs. The spirit that had kept me on the road for all those months, lent itself well to sleeping in tents with the tribes out in the villages. I didn't think there was much I couldn't handle or get through.

We spent Christmas in Nairobi, before heading out to the famous Treetops Hotel near Mount Kenya for a safari. It's the legendary site where Elizabeth was announced Queen of England after the death of her father King George VI, as well as having a long guest list of Hollywood celebrities. When we arrived at the entrance gate, the man in charge refused to let me go any farther. It was a mile hike to the actual location and seeing my wheelchair, he was not about to take on the liability. Galen and I assured him I could push my chair the distance; after all I had gone from Alaska to Washington, D.C. A short time on a dirt road in Africa was nothing.

"It is not you, young man, it is the wildlife. You won't be able to get away from the animals. You will be eaten!"

He probably didn't realize I could push my chair faster than most people can run. He finally consented, and there were no lions, or tigers or bears threatening me on the way to the lodge. Galen hoisted me on his back to get me up the stairs and inside the literal treetops. Built overlooking a watering hole, it has a spectacular bird's eye view of the wildlife.

Our next stop was Egypt to see the pyramids. Once again, I was the unexpected site for tour guides and tourists, people and passersby. And again, Galen and I showed determination to make whatever adaptations were necessary to get me down the road. We had two choices: camel or horseback. Because camels kneel down to be mounted, it was the accessible choice for me. My wheelchair was strapped to its back and I was lifted on easily. I wasn't quite prepared when the camel stood up, pitching me far forward as it shifted its weight to stand. We had a good laugh and a great adventure with Galen riding a horse just as unsteadily as I was on the camel.

On our way back to the states we stopped in The Netherlands, visiting Amsterdam and other local places of interest. It was a grand six weeks of adventure but it was time to get back to work and to training.

The Boston Marathon was just over

three months away.

"Everyone who competes in the games goes into strict training. They do it to get a crown that will not last; but we do it to get a crown that will last forever."

1 Corinthians 9:25 NIV

“Disability makes us different, but it does not make us less.”

Boston was *the* place to race for all serious athletes and competitors. It was the only marathon that required a qualifying time for participation. I raced the Philadelphia Marathon in November of 1988, if I did it again in ’89 it would be in time for me to qualify for Boston’s race scheduled the following April. But I knew the hills on its course, and I wasn’t going to risk not making a good finish. I specifically traveled half-way around the world to compete in Japan that October, knowing it was a course where I could achieve a qualifying time.

The Boston Marathon is the oldest continuous marathon distance race in the world. It sets the standard for all road marathon races. Twenty years before I was set to compete, a Vietnam Veteran named Eugene Roberts rolled up to the starting line on the cold, wet morning of April 20, 1970. He lost both legs when he stepped on a landmine 18 days after arriving in the jungles of South Vietnam. Using his hospital-issued wheelchair, he finished in just over seven hours paving the way for future disabled athletes. It still took five years before participants using wheelchairs were officially sanctioned.

The 94th running of the Boston Marathon in 1990 was one of the most competitive in the history of the race. There were close to 9,400 able-bodied participants with 46 "wheelies" registered. The *Challenge of a Lifetime* had built up my endurance and exposure to real road and weather conditions. I had competed several years in Paralympic sports as well as track and field events. I considered myself an athlete with challenges; in Boston I was a competitor among the most elite members in the field.

I felt ready.

The temperature was mild for April but the drizzling rain was going to make for challenges out on the course. Wet roads mean when you apply the brakes the tendency for the chair is to slide not slow down, plus your hands slip on the push rims. To assist with traction, athletes use ski wax. A dab of the gooey substance is placed on the chair. When you feel your hand starting to slip, you stick your thumb in it to regain your grip. It ruins your gloves and makes a mess of your wheels, but it gets the job done, and you have all the time you need on the other side of the Finish Line to clean up with WD-40 and alcohol.

The Marathon begins on Main Street, in Hopkinton, Massachusetts and for the first four miles it's all downhill; not bad for runners, but for guys in wheelchairs, it resulted in a catastrophic multi-chair crash in 1987. After the incident, significant changes were made, limiting the number of wheelchair entries as well as implementing a controlled start with a Pace Car to keep racers at a safer 15 mph pace.

The wheelchair athletes begin roughly 30 minutes before the Elite Men's group of runners. Even with the controlled start slowing us for the dangerous downhill, it doesn't take long to get rolling fast on the flatter stretches of the course.

Based on my qualifying time, I was in the third row back from the Starting Line. The rows consist of 7 chairs abreast, putting me in the center of the pack. As soon as the gun signaled the start, all 92 wheels were turning to quickly maneuver for a good position.

With my head down and close to my knees I wasn't watching what was ahead of me. I didn't realize my speed and quickly came up on the Pace Car. When I hit the brakes my wheels locked and Newton's First Law of Motion (an object in motion stays in motion with the same speed and in the same direction...) took over. Lucky for me, I was next to my friend and fellow US Track & Field teammate Joe Todisco, who saw me lift out of my chair. He tapped me on the shoulder, getting me back down to the seat, effectively executing the rest of Newton's Law, *unless acted upon by an unbalanced force.* He looked at me with a smile and said, "You're welcome."

In many marathons, the course will loop once or twice, but Boston is a *Point to Point* race. You start in Hopkinton, weave your way through 8 cities and towns and end at Copley Square surrounded by tens of thousands of cheering fans. All along the 26.2 miles, people are lining the route, holding up signs, and shouting encouragement. It keeps your adrenaline peaked.

At mile 16, coming into Newton I started up the long half-mile climb where the four Newton Hills crush the spirit of many athletes. It was time to push hard, dig deep and get prepared for the notorious last hill they call Heartbreak. I'd been racing for just over an hour, when the road started to wind and rise with a gut-grueling incline, heartbreak ahead! One of the revelers came alongside me with a beer in his hand yelling, "Push harder, come on push!" It worked, but it was probably more of my desire to get away from him, than any great motivational encouragement he offered. The next five miles is mostly all down hill, hard on runners but not too bad with wheels.

I crossed the Finish Line positioned between the Boston Library and the historic Old South Church, and placed in the top twenty. It was an exhilarating achievement that also qualified me for the September Pan American Games in Caracas, Venezuela.

The USA Wheelchair Track & Field coach heard I'd been to Africa. At the time, the international racing community was banning participants who had travelled to South Africa from competition. I assured her my itinerary did not include the apartheid state, and I was good to go.

As a kid in rural Pennsylvania, I'd grown up playing a wide variety of sports. I was good in most, but I excelled at track. For the Pan American games I competed in the middle and long distance track events, as well as the pentathlon. I had to learn how to throw discus, Javelin, and shot putt, but pushing in the meter races was a cinch.

In track, athletes work together on the course utilizing the aerodynamic principle of drafting. The person in the lead is essentially, exerting more effort breaking the wind and "pulling" those behind him along. It's considered good sportsman-like conduct for each person to take a turn in the lead, then pull out to let another athlete move forward to take their place pulling. This allows the lead athlete to then regain momentum and strength by drafting off the others. The more athletes racing the more rest you get. During the 5000 meter distance, the Mexican team stayed consistently behind me, but as I would move out of the lane to let one of their teammates take the lead, they never would, forcing me to pull, lap after lap without a break. The exertion was exhausting and aggravating. One guy stayed right on my wheels benefitting from my hard work, and strategizing where his position would be on the final lap, commonly referred to as the Bell Lap. With his head down focused only on the back of my wheels, he failed to realize I had come up on the slower athletes on the track. This time when I pulled out of the lap, he plowed right into the back of them crashing. He heard bells alright, but not at the finish line. Perhaps on his next race he took his turn, or looked where he was going.

After each event, the distances thrown and times run were calculated into points which determined the place of competitors. Even pulling the Mexican team behind me, I still had excellent track times and took home the Gold Medal.

I thrived in competition. Wheelchair sports gave me a way to feel active and like my old self. Most of those in the sport were former athletes that had suffered injuries causing their paralysis. We learned to compete in a new way, some very different than we experienced prior to being hurt. In between training and racing I continued my responsibilities at the golf course.

My next big event would be the 1991 World Games in Aylesbury, England. Traveling with that many athletes on a commercial airline was a challenge. The coaches had to coordinate getting us all into our seats, one by one down the aisles with a single transfer chair. Because there were so many of us, our wheelchairs all had to broken down, wheels removed and frames carefully stacked. Seventy or more wheelchairs take up a lot of room in the cargo bay. When we arrived, the more agile would make their way up the aisle hopping from seat to seat, get off and start putting the chairs together for the rest of us. It was generally a jumble of wheels, frames, and bodies seated on the floor of baggage claim as we figured out what wheels went with what chairs. Eventually, we'd roll around like a moveable jigsaw puzzle, examining the tires like detectives out to solve a mystery.

I'm not sure if it was the stress or just good old-fashioned forgetfulness that led to me misplacing my passport and not being able to travel with the team on our London flight. But by the day of competition the anxiety had passed and I placed 5th in my event. I was more excited than when I won the Gold Medal in Caracas. This ranking qualified me for the 1992 Paralympics in Barcelona, Spain. Based on how close we were in points at the World Games, I had a good chance at medaling.

Competitions were going well and I ramped up my training schedule with more weightlifting to increase the distance I was throwing the discus and shot putt. I continued to improve in pentathlon competitions and I was invited to the Olympic tryouts scheduled for late June. Since competing, tendon issues in my right elbow related to a high school injury flared up. When I increased my training the tendonitis got worse. One afternoon just before the tryouts, I felt a sharp twinge of pain in my elbow during my workout. I knew I did some damage when any movement I made was excruciatingly painful. A visit to the orthopedic doctor confirmed my fears, and I found out my tendon was starting to come apart. The only option for healing required rest and therapy.

After my motorcycle wreck I went to college and got a degree. I made an epic journey from Alaska to Washington, D.C. I helped transform a dairy farm into a golf resort. I traveled the globe and experienced more than most of my able-bodied friends. I competed with some of the best athletes in the world. I was living my life with a disability to the fullest. Para-Olympian Muffy Davis once said, "Disability makes us different, but it does not make us less.'

My walking days ended in August 1978,

my racing days—June 1992.

"He comes alongside us when we go through hard times, and before you know it, He brings us alongside someone else who is going through hard times so that we can be there for that person just as God was there for us."

2 Corinthians 1:4 The Message

FIRST TIME Skiing or Snowboarding?
Get your passport today!

"Decide for yourself if you want to race."

I was upset at not having the chance to try out for the Olympic team and the opportunity to travel to Barcelona, but I knew I needed to take time to let my tendon heal. I put the racing chair in the corner of the garage and replaced it with the latest in adaptive equipment at the time, a three-wheeled hand cycle which was not as hard on my joints. Work at my family's Moccasin Run Golf Club kept my time occupied and helped distract me from the disappointment.

By that winter, adapted skiing in the Northeast was gaining in popularity. I'd heard of an upcoming event in Breckenridge, Colorado called Ski Spectacular sponsored by Disabled Sports USA. I went to the event and found out that ski organizations were looking for adapted instructors to teach those with disabilities to ski. I took the classes, passed the test, and received certification as a PSIA (Professional Ski Instructors of America) Level 1 Adapted instructor. I made the transition from competitor to coach enjoying the opportunity to expose people with disability to the world of outdoor sports I loved.

Ski season ends as weather warms up for golfing. Before heading into the office, I'd be out on the road training. I worked more at the front counter than out on the grounds and got to know many of our regular customers personally. Early morning golfers would often see me and take a moment to talk before or after their round of play. It was after one of those morning routines while talking with Sam Much, he asked if I might help out a young girl in his neighborhood. I'd been retired from track racing for a few years so my response was, "I need to think about it," quietly hoping he'd forget.

Seeing the determination of the young 12 year-old as she pushed around the streets kept Sam asking, and asking if I had made a decision. He thought with my racing experience I should be able to help her out. Reluctantly, I agreed and went to meet the 7th grader at the local high school track course.

Amanda McGrory barely looked big enough to push around the track one time, let alone train to race competitively. She had contracted a viral infection at 5 years old which paralyzed her from the waist down. Our first year working together, was spent teaching her the basics of how to efficiently push a racing chair. I didn't push with her, but sat beside the track timing the lap intervals as well as providing encouragement, lap after lap, after lap. She had a good season of competition with the team in Philadelphia and thanked me for the help.

The following spring, she was a freshman in high school. She called to ask if I'd help her train again. It didn't take long before the progress she was making had me wanting to dust of my racing chair stashed in the corner of the garage. I was often invited along with her family to the Junior Track meets. I enjoyed seeing the competitions as well as being on hand to offer pointers and advice during the race. I was introduced to the coaches and other parents as her Coach. It was rewarding and exciting to be part of her development as a wheelchair track athlete.

One day as we started our workout on the roads and hills around the golf course, I sensed something was off. Up ahead was a mile-long hill I used for strength conditioning, and where I felt she needed improvement. Amanda wasn't pushing up to par as she normally did. To motivate her, I kept bumping into the backend of her chair telling her to pick up her speed.

Her head was buried in her knees to keep her weight and momentum in balance. Each time I bumped her chair, it threw the front end forward lifting her up in the air. I stopped when I heard her muffled cries. When we finished, she went straight to the car ready to be done for the day. Tim, her dad, came up to me and shared she wasn't sure if she wanted to keep track racing. She was doing well in basketball and was beginning to improve in that sport.

I asked if I might speak to her.

She was sitting inside the car, trying to contain her emotions. She refused to look at me, so I opened the door.

"Amanda, I love wheelchair sports and I am going to be out here pushing with or without you. I love to get out on the road, but that doesn't mean you need to do it. Decide for yourself if you want to race. Don't do it because I want you to or because your parents want you to. Do it because you want to. Call me when you're ready to push again."

Two days later she called.

I coached Amanda until she left for college. Every summer she competed in the Junior Nationals and soon started doing road races. She was getting notice from coaches that put together the Olympic team. When she was invited to the tryouts I encouraged her to go, reminding her not to worry about impressing anyone. "Just push your race."

She made the Developmental Team in 2004 and easily qualified for the 2008 Beijing Paralympics team. I was on a similar path when I made the Developmental Team in 1988 set to make the 1992 Olympic Team for Barcelona. But Amanda was younger and stronger and tendonitis didn't end her career. She went all the way, winning the Gold in the 5000 meter race, Silver in the marathon, and Bronze in the 800 meter race and 4 x 400 relay races.

Since Beijing, she has gone on to hold world records in the New York, Chicago, London, and Paris Marathons, and was a member of the 2012 USA Paralympic team. She'll go down in the history books as one of the elite women's wheelchair athletes.

Amanda made a choice. She chose not to let the difficulties of her disability keep her from excelling in competition. Accidents and illnesses happen in our lives that are unexplainable. Why did a 5 year-old girl wake up one day paralyzed? Why did a young man wreck his motorcycle in the mountains of Canada? There are questions we can ask about all the seeming injustices of the world. Even if we had the answers from heaven, the hills wouldn't be easier to climb, the rehab hospital hallways friendlier, or the sobs of a parent's cry softer.

When I came home from rehab I felt worthless. Every plan and dream I had hoped for was shaped around my being an able-bodied man. I was going to take over running the family dairy farm and see the world. At the time of my accident, I was secure in my faith and feeling blessed by God. I was surrounded by family, I had friends I enjoyed spending time with, I had a great church and loved the small town community I lived in.

Then a crash left me paralyzed,

then my grandfather died,

then my best friend died,

and then I got familiar with the cold, dark, hard place,

called Rock Bottom.

There are times when God looks cruel and life unfair. When I was in the depths of depression, the loving prayers of my family, friends and church gave me a lifeline to grab hold of. I choose to live and *boast all the more gladly about my weaknesses, so that Christ's power may rest on me* (2CORINTHIANS 12:9).

I learned to ask, "Why not me?" rather than "Why me?"

I learned to live with my disability.

"Now faith is the substance of things hoped for, the evidence of things not seen.

HEBREWS 11:1 NIV

"I am a person who lives with a disability, not a disabled person."

In the years that passed after *The Challenge of a Lifetime* I continued to find ways to motivate myself and others. When I could no longer compete, I got my certification to teach adaptive skiing. I reluctantly coached a young girl who was far from my image of a competitor, but who went on to win in the 2008 Beijing Paralympics. I was passionate to help others make empowering choices for their life, and I began to understand in a small way the sovereignty of God. What happens to me (good or bad) may be for the success, the benefit, or the faith of someone else. He can use me to influence the lives of those I come in contact with.

When the disability ministry of Joni Eareckson Tada opened an office in eastern Pennsylvania in 2000, my long-time friend Sib Charles asked me to be on the Board of Directors. Joni's life was an inspiration and I knew I could learn and grow professionally and personally with the organization. I'd been familiar with Joni since 1975 when she came to speak at my High School, three years before my accident. I was excited to get involved with the ministry and get back into speaking. It would be an opportunity to share how faith helped anchor me in the turbulent seas of living with paralysis.

In 1967, at 17 years old, Joni dove into the Chesapeake Bay and broke her neck, leaving her in a quadriplegic state, paralyzed from the shoulders down with minimal use of her hands. Joni taught herself to paint by holding a brush in her mouth and became an accomplished artist. She was recognized as a powerful motivational speaker and author of many inspirational books. Her influence on behalf of people with disabilities was renowned across the world. In 1979 she founded a ministry, and spent her life reaching out to the disabled community by organizing Family Retreats, developing church awareness programs, as well as distributing tens of thousands of wheelchairs to people living in impoverished nations.

I was still working at the Golf Course, but my involvement with *Joni and Friends* increased my interactions and influence in the disability community. It took me years to fully embrace, "I am a person who lives with a disability, I am not a disabled person." I was eager to impart that feeing to others.

In 2006, I became a part-time staff member, doing Disability Awareness seminars at churches on the weekends. I wasn't getting any younger, and I started to feel like my life needed a bigger purpose. I'd survived a life-altering injury, trained my body to compete in some of the biggest races in the world, gone on to have extraordinary adventures, but something was missing.

Spending time with people affected by disability rekindled the desires I had after my accident to be an influence among people overcoming the many obstacles of injury. When a full-time position at *Joni and Friends* was offered to me two years later, I didn't hesitate to accept. I saw this as my chance to impact others who were fighting with depression, guilt over the burden placed on family members, and anger at God; feelings I knew all too well. It became my mission to guide people on the journey towards spiritual healing. The job proved to be instrumental in my own emotional healing as well.

The year I turned 50, I didn't have a road map marking the milestone. There was no designated finish on some far distant Capitol steps. I didn't have a road crew or cheers from the sidelines encouraging me when I started to doubt. The emotional terrain was unfamiliar. In many ways I was pushing up mountains of feelings I'd grow comfortable pushing down.

As a young twenty-year old man, my attractiveness to the female population after my accident was one of my biggest fears. In high school I was an athlete, enjoying the attention of many of the girls in my class. But when I became a paraplegic, I wondered if anyone would ever be able to love me. Touring with the Choraleers did a lot to boost my faltering ego, as I realized girls still found me attractive. I can't deny I enjoyed the attention. However, my first serious relationship after my injury ended when I finished *The Challenge of a Lifetime.* From that point forward, my broken pride and wounded heart were held captive in a prison cage of doubt.

After almost 23 years love was about to set me free.

Sharyn Brautigan had been working with *Joni and Friends* since 1997. Through the years she had many roles in the organization and was currently opening the office in San Antonio, Texas. We met on several occasions at seminars even going on informal dates from time to time. The dilettante matchmakers at the company always commented we'd make a cute couple.

She wasn't just cute, she was beautiful. Her compassion and commitment to people living with disabilities was extremely attractive to me. This wasn't a woman who would be getting involved with me and then trying to figure out if she could handle the hardships. She'd been purposefully involved with people like me for over ten years. After the office opened, she was instrumental in launching a program for veterans and families returning from the Afghanistan and Iraq wars. Things were getting serious between us, and Sharyn committed to move to Pennsylvania. When I made the trip south during the Warrior Getaway weekend, there was no doubt in my mind I would ask her to marry me when she came up to find an apartment. I rolled into the relationship with the same energy and excitement that propelled me 5,605.8 miles!

2008 was a momentous year

I retired from my family's business after 20 years

I changed careers, accepting the offer at *Joni and Friends*

The little girl I coached would compete in the Beijing Olympics

I turned 50 in July

the 13th of August was the 30th anniversary of my last step

It was a lifetime (23 years) since I started the challenge in Fairbanks, Alaska.

I took a leap of faith

and married the love of my life.

"That's why we can be so sure that every detail in our lives of love for God is worked into something good."

ROMANS 8:28 THE MESSAGE

POWERED TO MOVE
WE WALK | WE ROLL | WE ROCK

"See where God is working and join Him there."

The sky was blacker than the asphalt on the street. The chill in the Brooklyn air distracted us enough to keep the butterflies fluttering in our stomachs manageable. Daylight Saving Time officially ended at 2:00 am, giving the more than 50,000 athletes participating in the New York City Marathon a much welcomed extra hour of sleep. It did not make it easier to board the first bus leaving the hotel at 3:00.

The sun wouldn't be up for another three and a half hours.

At the end of August, Chris Kaag, founder of *IM ABLE*, told me a spot was open on their team for the New York City Marathon. I'd been coaching him for the race, never considering I'd have an opportunity to participate. In the years when I was competing, it was an elusive dream. It seemed there was always a requirement, or injury that kept me out. Hearing Amanda McGrory's accounts allowed me to roll vicariously through the boroughs and bridges, the spectacular views, and the spectators of the iconic Marathon. She loved the race and I was finally getting a chance to share it with her.

There were a few other things I'd heard that were about to come in handy. As a push rim athlete, you want to be sure you're on the first shuttle headed to the Starting Line. The later the bus, the farther away they are forced to stop from the staging area. Not to mention navigating through thousands of able-bodied athletes pushing your racing chair in front of you while attempting to steer the chair you are settled in. That early in the morning, "Excuse Me" is as intrusive as the metal wheels moving through the masses of muscles.

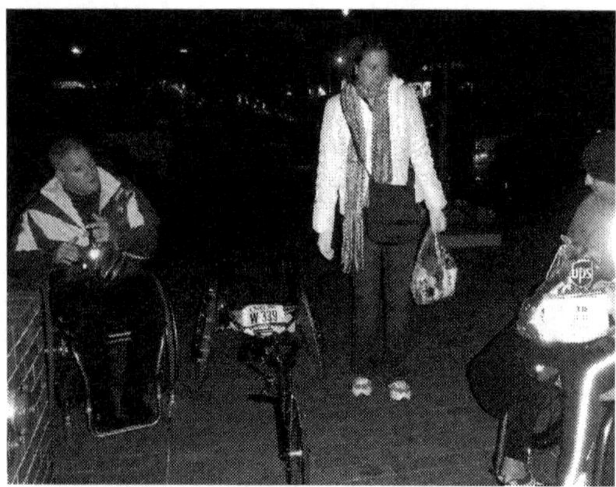

At the pre-staging area athletes transfer to their racing chairs as volunteers stand by to tag the regular chairs and transport them to the Finish Line. Only the top-ranked athletes have a designated place at the Start, for everyone else you are in the pack, wherever you can push for a place is about the only warm up you get.

It's a nightmare trying to get a bathroom break before the sound of the starting gun. By the time the sun rises over The Narrows and you're positioned on the Verrazano Bridge, it is what it is, and you are where you are.

Two million spectators line the course as it weaves through neighborhoods and across five bridges. It's a grueling 26.2 miles with the high-rises creating wind tunnels of resistance virtually every city block. The streets are uneven with potholes that can easily break a wheel and end your race.

When Chris and I got to the Staging Area he realized he had packed two left gloves. I gave him my right one, but he wouldn't take it. We taped his hands as best we could. He looked up and said,

"Don't wait for me."

I saw Amanda lining up with the pro women. It was a sweet reunion progressing from coach to comrade. It was the first marathon we were competing in at the same time. We encouraged one another for the race ahead of us both. I had done the oldest annual marathon (Boston) in 1990, I was about to take on the biggest at age 53, twenty-one years later.

> The familiar sound of the crowd was like a friend on the seat beside me.

All male athletes start before the females, even the professional women. This put me in front of Amanda. It didn't take long before she and the pack of female pros passed my position. I remember hearing the swift sound the aerodynamic wheels made coming up behind me. I looked back and saw her. For a brief moment I stopped pushing, as I watched the seemingly effortless grace of their movements.

It had been 14 years since I bumped the back of her wheelchair urging her to push harder on the hills. I felt terrible the day I made her cry, but I never felt prouder than the day she brought tears to my eyes on the streets of New York.

I finished well for my age at 2:31:30, but far behind my prodigy. The young girl that struggled on the small town roads in Pennsylvania, made history that day, setting the world record at 1:50:24.

When I trained for *The Challenge of a Lifetime,* I realized I could set achievable goals and accomplish significant things. The 5605.8 miles I pushed on the open road was the beginning of a journey that took me around the world in Paralympic sports, and on to coaching a record-breaking champion.

Becoming physically active changed my life and filled the emptiness I felt those first few years after my accident. In our work, Sharyn and I both regularly encountered individuals who shared they seldom go outside. They felt the same guilt I had about the effort, and the burden it placed on their family to take them on an "outing." I knew we could make a difference not just for the individual faced with the challenges of a disability, but we could also impact the family, giving them the opportunity to see their loved one enjoying themselves in a unique and supportive environment. We loved outdoor activities and we were ready to share that experience with the disabled community.

The idea to start a ministry of our own began when we participated in a race with *Athletes Serving Athletes.* Founders Dave and Sarah Slomkowski, enlisted able-bodied athletes they called "Wingmen" to push modified running joggers or racing push-chairs. Seeing the joy experienced by the kids and adults outside with the wind in their hair and smiles on their faces brought back memories from the 122 days I pushed across the country.

It felt like the sun breaking through a cloud covered day.

We talked with Dave and Sarah, and they fully supported our vision for ministry. We would include the developmentally and mentally disabled along with those with physical limitations. They graciously allowed us to utilize their training materials to get athletes prepared to serve the physically and mentally challenged.

We had a vision, now we just needed a plan.

My responsibilities at *Joni and Friends* were changing. I was leading teams to China for wheelchair distributions and International Family Retreats. It was a role I knew I could do from any home base. When I asked Ron Brautigan, Sharyn's dad, for her hand in marriage he agreed but also said, "You can get her out of Texas, but she'll want to come back." After enduring four Pennsylvania winters, she was ready to head south for warmer weather.

Sharyn pursued employment opportunities in Texas and relocated while I recovered from surgery to my shoulder. When I was finally able to join her, we started diligently pursuing getting the ministry off the ground. We decided to call it *Powered to Move* in reference to the able-bodied athletes who would be *powering* the challenged ones, and to honor our faith and acknowledge the real power behind our efforts.

As we moved forward in faith, the support we needed always seemed to come at just the right time. I had a meeting with John Maisel, Sharyn's boss at *East West Ministries International.* He offered us wonderful insight and encouragement into starting a ministry.

> "Step forth in faith, God will bless your efforts or teach you something in the process."

We were both ready to learn.

We began to serve alongside other local ministries to educate ourselves with as much practical information as we could. Cheryl Hood, the founder of *Victory Flows*, wanted us to meet the *Joni and Friends* international directors from Ghana, missionaries Allan and Patsy Fulton. It was fascinating to hear their journey of faith, missions and moving to Africa. They shared how the Bible Study *Experiencing God* had significantly influenced their lives and suggested Sharyn and I do the study as we planned the next steps to begin our own ministry.

The course was life changing. We were able to look back across the many seemingly disconnected events in our lives and connect them to what God planned and purposed for us to accomplish. One of the most impactful phrases, "See where God is working and join Him there," gave us the affirmation. *Powered to Move* was not only off the ground, we were rolling down the road.

We have never looked back.

"Although the Lord gives you the bread of adversity and the water of affliction, your teachers will be hidden no more; with your own eyes you will see them. Whether you turn to the right or to the left, your ears will hear a voice behind you saying, "This is the way; walk in it."

ISAIAH 30:20-21 NIV

"You need to come home."

There is a sound the wind makes in your ears when you are riding a motorcycle. The faster you go, the farther you ride the blending of motor and motion creates a kind of tactile symphony. The asphalt surface resonates through your body; the bumps, the rocks, all have a rhythm. And like a conductor's eloquent arms shaping the meter of the entire orchestra, your slight lean on the seat changes the course of a thousand pound machine.

I love the road's refrain.

My Dad always had a motorcycle. Some of my earliest memories are of the strength I felt in his arms as he hoisted me up to the seat of his bike, and him holding me between his legs on the gas tank as we drove away from my kindergarten. I was never scared, my Dad had me, and he'd never let anything bad happen.

But something bad did happen.

On Friday, February 7, 2014 my father suffered a major stroke. My mother made the call to say, "You need to come home." I decided to drive from up from Texas, since no one could say if it would be a matter of days or longer. Sharyn planned to fly up as soon as I was able to tell her news of his condition. It was a long and lonely road trip with time for reflection.

My father and I never had a conversation about August 13, 1978. During those first months home after the accident, when I was sinking into depression, the unacknowledged and unspoken guilt disabled *him* to the point he couldn't help my mother with me. From time to time his whispered anguish would be heard, "I never should have let you go on that trip."

It haunted him.

For years, anytime it would come up I attempted to reassure him with, "It wasn't your fault." I'm not sure he ever forgave himself for enjoying motorcycles, and setting the example to his sons of fun from the speed of two wheels.

My parents met me in St. Louis during the *Challenge of a Lifetime.* I always thought it helped my Dad. He was able to witness my determination, the enjoyment I had on the road, and speaking to groups at hospitals and churches. He saw I was not helpless; and although in those days, people in wheelchairs were called *cripples*, he had evidence across 5,605.8 miles of concrete to break the stereotype that disability makes you weak.

My life has been punctuated by tragic interruption, as well as triumphing adventures. I was permanently paralyzed at twenty years old, but I am the only person in the world that traveled the Alaska Highway in a wheelchair.

I was an athlete before and after my injury.

Up until I arrived in Lancaster, my father had been non-responsive. He was constantly surrounded by family members, my mother, my brothers, and four of his grandchildren. His brothers arrived on Monday and it seemed as if he was holding on to allow them a final goodbye. That evening, after my brother Curt's kids left, we were together again, singing hymns signaling an important event was taking place; only this time it wasn't Christmas, Easter or Sunday morning, it was my Dad's "Home-going."

His breath became shallow, he opened his eyes, and we all saw the face of a healthy robust man. He didn't look sick anymore. He looked like the dad we always knew; the one who swept me up in his arms and put me on top of his motorcycle taking me home from kindergarten feeling like Superman.

No one can say what happens when a soul passes from this life into the next. However, the Bible tells us in the twelfth chapter of Hebrews we are surrounded by a great cloud of witness. Those who have gone before are cheering us on, encouraging us to run the race with endurance. (Hebrews 12:1-2).

For years, I held on tight to the last words my Papa Zook spoke to my mother before he died. Perhaps those were some of the first words my Pop heard when he arrived.

"See, I told you Mike was going to be alright."

Epilogue

"I long to accomplish a great and noble task, but it is my chief duty to accomplish small tasks as if they were great and noble."

HELEN KELLER

Powered to Move participated in our first official race April 12, 2014, two months after we laid my father to rest. Our vision to include athletes with physical and intellectual disabilities was realized as well as entering with two in adaptive running joggers. They crossed the Finish Line with arms raised in victory alongside their five able-bodied Wingmen.

Since that time we have provided adaptive equipment grants for athletes, trained over 70 *Wingmen*, and the races and medals are too numerous to name. Our future is to have Racing Clubs in multiple locations where people with disability can unite hand in hand, or arms on adaptive equipment with able-bodied athletes to get out, run, race, or roll and have fun. They might be "small tasks" to the accomplished athletes we partner with, but it is indeed for a noble cause.

We have big goals because we serve a big God!

The Diary of Dorothy King

THE FOLLOWING IS A DIRECT TRANSCRIPTION

On August, 13 1978 my mother began to keep an account of what happened regarding my accident and the immediate days following.

She knew she would want a record of God's faithfulness.

Her notes were personal. You will see included many names of people in our community of faith who offered prayers and support those initial days up until I was transported home a little over two weeks later on August 29. To honor that community, my mother's faith, her prayers, her commitment and unwavering hope—I include it here.

You have read my story but, in more ways than I can understand this side of heaven, this is also an acknowledgement of those prayers, and the hours spent by my bedside trusting and believing God for a miracle. Thirty-seven years ago, the miracle looked like "believing I would walk" again. Today, I can say, the *miracle* is the life I live WITH my disability, ministering to thousands of people across the world with a message of hope, sharing the Salvation offered through trust in Jesus Christ. I thank God for knowing the bigger picture, and for my mother who believed in Him!

I would not be the man I am today if not for her.

Sunday August 13

Mike called us around 2:00 from near Banff Alberta Canada to report they were having a good trip and wanted to know how things were going at home and about PaPa's condition. At 7:00 that evening, just as we were ready to leave for church, the phone rang and it was Gregg Petersheim to report to us that Mike was involved in an accident and was seriously injured. He said he would call back at 10:00 that night to report more after they knew more. So we went to church and shared our need and they gathered around us and laid hands on us and offered special prayers. After church Larry (Kennel) Bill (York) and Bonnie (York) came along home with us and were here with us when we received more from the hospital concerning Mike's injuries. The report was that Mike had both legs broken, broken ribs and internal injuries and bleeding, broken back and paralysis from the waist down. Wow!

What a message.

Bill and Bonnie and Larry prayed with us and we tried to pull ourselves together enough to dwell on scripture and claim them and we told the Lord that Mike is His child to heal as he sees best. As Rod, Curt, Kent, Wendel, Paul and I were praying and crying together we were about to go to bed 12:15 AM, David and Rhoda and Kevin King were at the door. As we talked awhile we decided to try and made plane reservations for the next morning. So they stayed awhile and we finally got reservations for the next morning at 9:40 AM out of Philadelphia. David said he would take us down the next morning. The boys than went to bed but Paul and I shared some scriptures and prayed together. Then at 1:00 AM the phone rang and it was Dr. Cochran from Foothills Hospital in Calgary saying that Mike is much worse and they will have to operate immediately on the internal injuries. We talked awhile and then told the Dr. we would be praying for them while operating. We also told him we had arrangements made to fly out and would be arriving at around 3:15 that PM. He said that was great and that he would tell Mike that we are coming. Dr. Cochran said he would call us back through the night if Mike's condition got any worse. Paul and I again fell on our knees and cried out to the Lord for mercy and help, Psalms 46:1. We prayed all night and it was really hard work. We ask the Lord to guide the surgeon's hands and PTL (*Praise the Lord*) He did just that, for the doctors told us Monday afternoon when we arrived that when they got to working on him it wasn't quite as bad as the X-rays showed. Well we told them that we were in prayer for them and they thanked us.

We left for the airport at 7:30 AM and David unloaded us and left and we went to get our tickets. We were flying United and when we choose a line to stand in to get our tickets the lady typed on the computer and then turned to us and said, "You are the people whose son was in an accident". And we said we were. She then turned to us and said, "I don't know how religious you people are but in a time like this God can and will take care of you". And we said Amen and lifted our Bibles up for we decided to not pack them in the suitcase but carry them with us so we could read, pray and meditate on the plane. Well she assured us that she would be praying for us. So how did that happen or did God plan that we get in her line waiting for our tickets? I know God planned that for us for it is just what we needed at that hour of waiting there alone. PTL.

We boarded the plane and flew to Denver. The man sitting beside us saw us reading our Bibles and ask if we are Christians, so we shared with him our need and he promised us he would be praying and also share at his church and they too would be in prayer. We waited in Denver about an hour and then flew Western into Calgary. While waiting in Denver we meet a couple from West Liberty, Ohio. Hostetter was their name and after sharing where we were all going and why they told us they would be in prayer for us. How wonderful to belong to the family of God, no matter where you go you can identify with Gods family. PTL. We did arrive in Calgary at 3:15

Monday PM August 14

We were tense because we did not know whether Mike would be dead or alive, for we were in a foreign land and felt all alone at the moment. After going through customs and getting our baggage there were the three boys Gregg, Merv and Ron, and Nathan Stoltzfus from Morgantown, to meet us. PTL. The boys told us immediately that Mike was doing well considering conditions and they took us to the hospital. As soon as we got to the hospital, 9th floor, we met the Doctors, so we stopped and talked to them. They were super nice to us and explained everything concerning his condition to us. They said he is very ill and will take a long time to mend and concerning his paralysis they feel is permanent damage. Well, we thanked them for what they are doing but also told them we believe in God and are expecting a miracle from him. They then took us to Mike's room and our hearts were broken and crushed as we stood by his broken body. He opened his eyes when I called his name and said,

"Hi Mom."

Tears came to my eyes and I thanked the Lord for sparing his life and praised Him for the healing I know He is yet going to bring to his broken body. He had tubes on both sides of his rib cage pumping out the blood, internal bleeding, Tube in his nose to his stomach, Oxygen mask on, catheter, an incision 8" on each leg between the knee and thigh to mend his broken legs, another incision 8 to 10 inches long on his stomach to mend the internal injuries, but worse of all his strong body not able to move, the paralysis. This was really difficult for me but again and again I told the Lord that Mike is His child to take or leave, whatever will bring Him the most glory.

Then that scripture came to my mind in Psalms 139:13-18 how our bodies are wonderfully made and how the Lord knit all the inner parts of our bodies together and I just said thank-you Lord, for I felt that was a promise to me that He was again going to do that to Mike's broken body. PTL, Mike slept a lot or at least had his eyes shut a lot, but he was in a lot of pain, but never once did I hear Mike ever complain or moan with pain or anything. The Lord gave him patience to bear it and had mercy on him. PTL. We stayed there at the hospital till about 7:30 that evening and then walked about a mile to the motel where the boys made a reservation for us for the night. Paul and I decided we were going to fast and pray we didn't know for how long. So when we got to our room we again opened our Bibles and by this time the Lord had shown us many promises, especially in Psalms 34, 37, 40 and many more.

We prayed together and cried together and asked the Lord to please give us rest, which he did. PTL.

Tuesday August 15

We had made out the night before to meet in the boy's room the next morning for a time of sharing and praying together at 9:30. This was a blessed time together. These boys were so concerned about Mike and we gathered in a circle, joining hands and prayed together.

This was really strength to Paul and I.

Then Paul and I walked over to the hospital and immediately went in Mike's room. He was in constant care so we did have to check with a nurse before entering. Mike seemed a bit brighter but was in a lot of pain yet.

Mike does not know at this time yet the extent of all his injuries.

The Dr. said not to tell him more than he would ask, because his body is in tremendous shock and its best for him to not be told until he would ask. The Dr. said in 24 hours he would know if his paralysis is permanent. We were in prayer much concerning this. Many phone calls were starting to come for us. Amos Stoltzfus, Ron's father from Minnesota called several times. Merle Embleton from Delaware called and wondered if he could do anything. We told them all to pray. Ron was leaving for his home this morning so we met with the boys in the waiting room and had prayer together before he left. Gregg and Merv were going to stay all week. We got a note from the business office that they wanted to see us. They wanted 10 day advance payment $2000.00 dollars immediately. Well this was another prayer request for they didn't want to work with Mike's insurance company, for they wanted payment right away. Well this took some phone calls back home and that evening Paul and I made it a matter of prayer and asked the Lord to work it all out for us. Well within 24 hours our prayer was answered. We were able to move into the hospital motel this evening which was another answer to our many prayers, for it was a lot cheaper for us. We reserved it for a week and it was so handy. This hospital was very modern and big. It was 13 stories high with 2 floors underground. They had their own motel for out of town people. When Paul and I went to our room that evening we again spent time in prayer and we were fasting. I woke up through the night and had a real picky, burning feeling on the bottom of my feet and I shouted PTL and claimed that for Mike. I feel the Lord allowed me to experience that to tell me that someday Mike is going to experience that. PTL. Paul also woke up one night with extreme pain across his chest, also feeling that the Lord allowed him to have that pain to identify with Mike with all his chest pains.

We again asked the Lord to give us rest which he did.

We did call home to the boys to check on them and it was so encouraging to hear them say everything is going fine and that they are praying for Mike and us too. PTL for wonderful boys. Arnold and Maietta Moshier also called this evening just to encourage us and showed there concern for Mike.

Wednesday August 16

Today it rained all day. Mike had a smile when we walked in his room this morning. We talked with Doctors Taylor and Cochran and they said Mike will never walk again that the paralysis is permanent as far as they can tell. We thanked them for what they did and told them that we are trusting God for a miracle. Doctor Taylor said you must be Christians and we said Amen we are, and he said he is too. So PTL for Christian Doctors, Like Taylor. He is a wonderful man.

We went down to the chapel to be alone, they have a chapel on the ground floor of the hospital that is open 24 hours a day for anybody to use when they want to be alone and meditate or pray, so Paul and I spent a lot of time in there each morning and throughout the day. So we went down there to pray and be alone with God. We Prayed, "Dear God I need more faith to believe that You will heal Mike, in Your own time and way. Matthew 18:19, John 15:7". The doctors also talked to us on what we plan to do with Mike. Will we keep him there or transfer him back home. Well, we needed help on this so again we made it a matter of prayer, for we wanted to do what was best for Mike.

Pastors Paul Landis and Jake Weibe stopped in to see us. Herman Glick (our pastor back home) called Linford Hackman and he in turn called Paul Landis at Carestairs, about 50 miles north of Calgary. They were a real blessing from the Lord. We had them go in to see Mike and then Jake Weibe invited us to stay at their home in the city of Calgary. We accepted and thanked the Lord for meeting that need, for it did get very expensive to stay in the motel every night. He said he would come back about 9 o'clock to pick us up. PTL he met our needs again. Flowers came today from Steve Smoker and Nate King. We showed them to Mike but he wasn't allowed to have anything in his room, so I took them along to the Weibe's and kept them in our room.

Dr. Dykstra, one of the doctors that worked on Mike on the chest area took an interest in us and Mike and he offered to go get Mike's motorcycle and store it in his garage for the moment until we decided what to do with it. So this evening Gregg and Merv went along with Doctor Dykstra about 80 miles in his station wagon and brought the wrecked motorcycle back to his place and stored it in his garage for the time being.

Quite a kind gesture I'd say.

The doctor was telling us that his wife was getting a bit concerned for the doctors cannot get involved like this with their patients or they would never be home. So Doctor Dykstra told his wife that this case was different, that he was impressed with these people and he wanted to help us for we were so many miles from home. So she said ok. Paul quoted that scripture in Psalms somewhere "Some trust in chariots but we trust in God." Since we had reservations in the hospital motel yet we told the Weibe's we would wait till tomorrow night to move over to their house, so we were with Mike awhile in the evening and had prayer with him before leaving and then went to our room. We again called the boys at home and they said PaPa was not feeling so good and they would have to operate.

Thursday August 17

This morning we checked out of the motel and Jake Weibe came over and picked up our luggage. He was coming back at nine that evening to pick us up then. We went to Mike's room and his lung was filling up considerably and they were draining it. They were going to give him a spinal dye type of test today to determine if fluid was dripping out of the tip of his spine, which would be more trouble if that was the case. Well PTL that was not the case. Dr. Cochran told us the end of the spine had sealed over and all the fluid is coming from the internal bleeding and they would have to keep the tubes in for a while yet. Mike did not look as good today perhaps due to all the bleeding and spinal test. He was very short of breath too, so they were working on his chest area a lot and draining the lungs, because of being so close to the heart.

Paul had very severe chest pains today at times and he felt the Lord gave it to him to feel a bit what Mike is bearing. I thanked the Lord for that same Spirit and Power that raised Christ from the dead was available in us, dwell in me. Last night Aldie called to tell us that at 8 o'clock that night they were going to be in special prayer for Mike and that we should be with Mike at that time too which would have been 6 our time, and that we should lay hands on Mike and be in prayer.

So Paul asked the head nurse if this would be possible to be at Mike's bedside at that time and he told her why and she said it would be fine. Well, this word must have gotten around, for the next day Dr. Cochran even asked us how it worked out for us and also the head nurse ask if it worked out ok. They really seem to care too. We found out later that many churches stopped at 8 o'clock at their prayer meetings and fell on their knees in prayer especially for us. PTL for brothers and sisters in the Lord who hurt when we hurt enough to spend time in prayer like that. Merv, Gregg, Paul and I were in around Mike's bed and we all prayed and I sang a song softly and we were really in an attitude of prayer.

It was really up lifting for us.

Menno Epp from the Foothills Mennonite Church came by to see us today. He found a place for Gregg and Merv to stay too. The community really seems to care and want to help. Dr. Taylor spoke to us today about arranging an air ambulance to transport Mike home when he is ready. The Doctors felt the best thing for Mike would be to transport him home to familiar surroundings for the next steps of recovery and this would be concerning the back. So Paul and I looked into this and started getting some information. Another bouquet came from Mike's Sunday school class (Aldie and Judy) and Carol Burkhart and Joanne Umble. Again we showed them to Mike and then took them back to the Weibe's with us.

Jake was there to pick us up at 9 and we went to their home. We met for the first time Elsie, Jake's wife and their two children, Linda 6, and Brian, 3. We had a room and bath in the basement. It was so cold and we did not have any sweaters along. It was so hot when we left home never thinking how far North we were going. Elsie offered us something to drink which we accepted and then retired for the night. We were unusually tired but slept well.

Again the Lord was good to us.

We did call home again to the boys. They seem so concerned and say everything is going well. I called to Anna's (my sister) today at noon for this was Wendel's 8th birthday and we wanted to wish him "Happy Birthday" Anna said they were considering operating on Dad.

Friday August 18

This is the day the Lord hath made, I will rejoice and be glad in it. We had breakfast at the Weibe's, but we told them all we wanted was juice, coffee and toast, for we were not eating. Rodney called before we left Weibe's this morning to tell us that we should check at the bank at the hospital for the money was wired up. Jake took us to the hospital at 9 and we went directly to Mike's room. He looks brighter today.

He's beginning to ask us questions now.

He asked me if we talked to the doctors about the fact that he can't move his legs. I answered him, "Yes we did." Then he asked if they think he will be able to move them soon. And I said it will take time to heal and they don't know yet. He was satisfied with that. Then later in the day he asked if he could sit up and I told him his back is injured too severely to sit up yet and he was again satisfied with that answer. Gregg and Merv are in and out every day too. Mr. Berry and his wife came by to see him. This was the man that administered first aid at the scene of the accident. He seemed to have pride in what he did but we also PTL for the fine job he did for according to how it would have been handled it could have been fatal.

Paul says today that his legs feel so weak. He feels the Lord is allowing all of this so he can bear with Mike. Rodney called again this evening to say that Nate and Parke are considering coming out to pick up the motorcycles. We warned them that it is far and would be a big trip. They said they know. Arnold Moshier also called again this evening. They have really been a blessing to us and Mike. Oh, we did go to the bank and pick up the $2000.00 and then to the office to pay the 10 day advance. This really made them happy.

Saturday August 19

Herman called this morning at Weibe's to tell us that the church is really behind us and want to help us. Paul called Nate and told him not to come for the bikes. We went to the hospital and Mike seemed brighter again today. He started eating today for the first time and they pulled the IV out. The nurse washed his hair today, how nice. Looks like Mike again. Mike seemed uncomfortable at times today.

He never complains so I'm not sure what hurts.

Wish I could do something for him for he says he is bored. Larry and Marilyn Kennel called this PM at the hospital and Shirley and Mav Yoder were there so they talked too. We also looked into some air ambulance and such prices. They want over $8000.00 to fly him Leer Jet, direct flight, 4 hours, to Harrisburg. We feel we can't afford that. Mike had tears when we told him Calvin Yoder is taking this hard and doing some serious thinking. Also PaPa had surgery yesterday and is doing fine. Says he prays for Mike every day, many times. Jake was there to pick us up again. We have learned to know them better now and really enjoy being with them a short time in the evening.

Sunday August 20

We got up early and Jake took us to the hospital so I could feed Mike his breakfast and then Jake picked us up and we went along with them to their church. Jake is pastor of the First Mennonite Church in Calgary. They are GC Mennonites. Their church is made up of a lot of older people who are known as the Russian Mennonites. Many of them immigrated from Russia into Canada. They speak German and broken English and are really dear people. They showed so much love and concern to us. Jake asked if we would give our testimony and share something with the people, so we said we would.

It was really difficult but we both did.

When we came back and sat down an old, dear lady sitting in the front of us reached back and laid a ten dollar bill on my lap. I just had to cry and we thanked her. We told her the Lord will surely be pleased to bless her for sharing, who knows, maybe her last ten dollar bill, for she was a dear old widow lady. We talked with many people after church and then Jake took us back to the hospital where we found Mike looking a bit brighter. We feel everyday he is moving forward in his recovery but it always hits me to think he is paralyzed. I fed him dinner and he seemed to enjoy it. He doesn't eat much but enough. This afternoon seemed rather long I don't know really why, more than I think we were really homesick.

We called to Paul's home where we knew the boys were for dinner, so we got to talk to them, plus Nate's were there too. They reported everything going fine but seem a little homesick too. Jon Kent Witmer called to ask about Mike and Chris Slabaugh also called. We reported all this to Mike. Arnold Moshier also called to say how he called the people at Roxbury where Choraleers gave a program the week end Mike left on the trip and they remembered him and Arnold sent them a picture of Mike and they took it to their prayer meeting that following Wednesday night and gathered around his picture, laying hands on it and praying for him.

They felt the Lord saying that Mike will walk again someday. PTL

Its reports like these that really lift Paul and I up and helps us trust more on the Lord and not on our feelings. We had prayer with Mike and then left for the Weibe's again. Also Gregg and Merv were at the Foothills Mennonite Church that Sunday morning and they too found a good hearty welcome and concern for Mike.

Paul and I have had many nights—I guess you would call them "Dark nights of my soul." We finally came to a place where we could tell God that we wanted HIS presence in our life more than we needed the understanding of all the circumstances around us. You see there were times when we just felt we couldn't understand all that was happening.

Monday August 21,

This morning Mike looked good and I knew something good must have happened. Well they pulled the tube on the right side, and this was good news. Gregg and Merv came in early today for they are making plans to fly home. They plan to leave tomorrow morning. I assisted Mike again today on his eating. He must lie flat on his back without lifting his head up so eating is a bit difficult. We talked to Doctor Taylor again today and we asked if he has any idea when Mike could be moved and he said maybe not for 10 days yet.

We were a bit disappointed by that.

Mike's condition is improving but slowly. He is aware by now how serious his condition is. He doesn't talk about it but I'm sure he thinks plenty. We again looked into some possibility of transporting him home and WOW! Such prices. We also contacted Hershey Medical Center on transferring him there. Things are working out for that transfer. PTL. Prices were $4000.00 commercial or $8000.00 Leer Jet. Don't know if we can swing that.

We really had peace about it though for we knew the Lord would make a way for us.

It was a beautiful day today. We can see the Canadian Rockies right from Mike's hospital room. They are just beautiful. They were snowcapped over the weekend. We both are fed daily on God's word, no appetite for the natural food.

Mike seems very uncomfortable at times.

The tubes tend to irritate and hurt when the bleeding slows down and the tubes get dry. We had prayer again and left for the day. Today seemed long again. We called home to the boys and things are going good they say PTL, and they mowed hay today.

Tuesday August 22

Mike had a big smile for us again this morning so I said PTL what has happened. He said they are coming in soon to pull the other chest tube. This meant he was completely healed from the internal bleeding. PTL. Doctor Taylor said he is doing fine, make final plans to move him home. This was exciting news so we worked on transporting him again. This was the discouraging part, for no commercial flights wanted to bother with a stretcher patient at this time, too busy. Some more excuses were, this might upset the other passengers, this would take up too many seats, we don't really have time to bother with a stretcher, etc. So Paul and I went to the chapel to bring our need before the Lord and also thank and praise Him for what He has already done.

We really cried out before the Lord and really felt a peace and protection about it all.

Also we talked to Doctor Dykstra today and he asked if he could accompany us home if a doctor needs to go along. This was a real direct answer to prayer because Doctor Dykstra was one of the many doctors who worked on Mike's case the whole time and who would know him better, his condition, and all, better than Doctor Dykstra. Also this was the doctor who brought Mike's wrecked cycle to his garage and we just felt he really cared about us, for he came in and out every day, several times a day. So we really felt good about this.

We got as phone call today from Wendell Umble, and he was over at the airport and was stopping over to see us. Well, we knew the Lord sent him to us for we shared our need about flying Mike home and him being a pilot said he would help us on this, in fact he said just don't worry about this I will work something out for you.

You see Air Canada was at this point threatening a strike, and they were the only ones at this point, after much persuasion said they would take us. Well, we had a good long visit with Wendell and it was so good to talk with him. We had prayer together with Gregg and Merv and they left for home. We appreciated what they did for us all by staying there all week.

Mike asked us today if we think he will ever have feeling again in his legs. WOW!

What should I say.

We had prayer with him and again left for the night. Back at the Weibe's Krista Miller, Mike's girlfriend called to ask about him.

Wednesday August 23

I talked to Anna again today and Dad seems worse, not due to his operation but failure of kidneys and bladder now. Poor man, he is so discouraged. Herman Glick called this morning at Weibe's. Just wanted to tell us everyone is concerned about what's happening. Rodney also called to ask Dad some things about the farm. We finally got to the hospital and told Mike Krista called. It seemed to please him. Mike is beginning to get some mail now. Paul called Doctor Weiss (family doctor in Pennsylvania) at noon and set up final arrangements for Mike's transfer to Hershey Medical Center. He said they are all ready for him whenever we can come. We said we would keep in touch on that.

It is raining outside again today.

Wendell called to tell us he can help us on arrangements for flying home. PTL, another answer to prayer. Also Doctor Taylor called Hershey Medical Center and talked to another doctor there just to inform him on what to expect.

Today they moved Mike out of constant care to another room. He has 3 roommates and it is much nicer. Paul went to the chapel to pray while I fed Mike his supper. Paul and I shared a bowl of soup this evening. Linford Hackman and his wife stopped in today to visit us. This was the first time we ever met them and what a blessed visit we had. We read the 34th Psalm to Mike, and Paul and I had dwelt on that every day for it met our needs.

Thursday August 24

Linford Hackman called us at the Weibe's home this morning. He just wanted to tell us they would be in prayer for us. Also the Air Canada airlines called to confirm a flight for Monday morning. When we got over to the hospital Wendell called too to tell us he had it all set up for Monday morning with Air Canada and he would be down on Sunday to see us and give us the tickets. Again we thanked the Lord for he is so good. We saw doctors Taylor and Cochran and we told then our plans and they both agreed that it would be ok that Mike is in good shape. I called my Dad at the hospital to talk to him and he sounded so weak and discouraged.

I felt so bad after I hung up.

I also talked awhile to mother and she was very discouraged too. I guess everything together put a lot of pressure on them. This afternoon, Jake and Elsie and the children picked us up and took us out to Banff and we bathed in the hot springs. What an experience. This was natural water coming down off the mountain into a big swimming pool and the temperature of the water was 103 degrees and it felt plain down hot, but good. We stayed in about 30 minutes and when we got out we felt all weak. It just drains you of all your strength but is really good for relaxing and arthritis. The drive was just beautiful.

This was near where the accident happened.

Mike had visitors while we were gone; Paul Landis and Menno Epp were in to visit him. Paul and Susanne Landis were in earlier in the week to visit too and they invited us up to Carestairs to their home sometime. In the evening the Penners, where Gregg and Merv stayed came over to see us. Also Jake came early to pick us up and came to visit Mike. We all had prayer together and then left for another day.

Friday August 25

This morning Elsie fixed some fresh fruit for Mike. He really enjoyed it. We talked with Doctor Dykstra this morning and he said he is all set to go along with us. Different nurses were saying they wanted to go along too. Also Wendell called this morning to say everything was in shape for Monday morning. Wendell was a Godsend to us.

Paul and I spent time down in the chapel this morning alone with God. We had prayers of thanks and also a time of quiet to allow God to speak to us.

What a challenge. In the afternoon Wendell called to say Air Canada went on strike and it was all off for Monday. Even though they possibly could settle it before Monday they would not want to bother with this stretcher patient. Wendell expressed he is sorry but will try to work on something else.

God had told us in the chapel that morning to trust, delight and commit, taken from Psalms 37 so we again committed everything over to him and we tried not to worry. But again I knew my dad was getting worse every day and I wanted to get home. This was a beautiful day outside and they asked Mike if he would like to go outside for a while. He said sure, so guess what, they pushed him outside, bed and all and he laid out there in the warm sun.

We couldn't believe they would do such a thing, for it was right out front where everyone drove up to the front doors and people were in and out all the time. It sure makes for an interesting story.

I sure wished for a camera.

Mike's camera was the only thing that was missing from all his belongings, so we don't know if it was lost at the scene of the accident or what. He stayed outside for a half hour and seemed to really enjoy it. An elderly man from Weibe's church stopped in to see Mike, Epp was his name. Back to the Weibe's for another night and watched the news and it didn't sound good for the air strike, but again we gave it to the Lord and we plan to leave it there. PTL.

Saturday August 26

We arrived at the hospital and talked to Mike about the air strike and he seemed disappointed too. Paul and I went to the chapel to pray and meditate again.

God told us to let go and let God arise.

What a challenge again today. Wendell called later in the day to tell us that Air Canada was off. No flights for weeks out of Calgary. He said he could fly us out of Canada into Great Falls, Montana in one of his planes if the doctors give their consent. We said we would talk it over with the doctors and he said he would be calling back later. When Wendell called back Doctor Dykstra happened to be right there at the desk so we just had him talk to Wendell and Doctor Dykstra said that should be no problem, go ahead and plan for that and forget about Air Canada. PTL again he takes care of everything and does it right.

This PM they wheeled Mike outside again.

The sun felt so good to him and it was a most lovely day and warm. Tonight Jake and Elsie and children are coming for us at 8:00 to pick us up for they want to take us down town and climb the huge tower to look out over the city of Calgary. It is a huge city but beautiful. It was a lovely view of the city. Back to Jake's and Jake's brother and his family arrived for the weekend. We were hoping to be on our way home by now but didn't happen. So the Weibe's really had a house full. Other people offered to house us but Jake's wanted us to stay, so we did.

Sunday August 27

This morning Menno Epp picked us up and we went to the Foothills Mennonite Church. We had another beautiful experience. We again were ask to give our testimonies. We had a wonderful opportunity to thank the people for what they are doing for us.

It made us feel at peace to know they were praying for us and the love and concern they showed to us.

So many people ask us out to dinner but we promised Mike we would be right over after church. This being another beautiful day they wheeled Mike outside again. Jake came by to take his picture and another couple we met in the morning at church and he brought some oil along and anointed Mike that afternoon right outside in the sunshine.

It was a wonderful experience.

Also Jake brought his recorder and had Mike give his testimony while he recorded it and then took it back to their Youth group and played it for them. At 4:30 this afternoon someone is coming by the hospital to take us to Carestairs and we had a good supper with the Landis's. Then to their little country church. We had a blessed time together sharing and again the love and concern they showed to us for they gave us a love gift of $157.00. PTL.

Paul and Susanne Landis took us back to Calgary then after the meeting. We really had a good time being with them. We arrived back at Jake's about 10:30 and sat there and talked yet for another hour or more.

Monday August 28

Again Jake took us to the hospital. Our plans are to go home tomorrow morning. Doctor Dykstra seems excited too and ready to go. We are really excited about going but Lord; we must have your guidance and blessing. Thanks to the Lord for Wendell Umble for he just took care of planning it all and I'm sure he had connections that we could never have gotten through like he did. In fact he called to tell us that his plane has been called out, the one he was planning to use, so he let it go and he got us another one, bigger and better. So he chartered one through a friend and he would still go along but would not be piloting the plane.

Also Kerry Munro, another Godsend, came down to see us for he is coming to Mount Joy Pennsylvania, to the Jay and Martha Garber farm to work a few weeks and he offered to bring all the motorcycles along. Wow!

What another answer to prayer.

So he came down to see where the cycles were stored so that when he is ready to come he could pick them up and be on his way. He was planning to come sometime soon after Labor Day, which wasn't far off. Jake stopped by this afternoon and handed us $2410.00 in Canadian cash which his church gathered together in the service yesterday Sunday offering.

This is unbelievable.

Here is a church that has never met us before but hurt with us through this experience and wanted to share their blessing with us. O Lord, I prayed, be pleased to bless these dear people. Words will never express our innermost feelings through this act of love and kindness.

Well, again the Lord met our need for we would have to have money wired up again to finish paying our bill at the hospital, for we were leaving in the morning. So we went right down to the office and finished paying off our hospital bill with this offering plus we had enough to pay all the ambulance stops at the airports on the way home. PTL. We paid our hospital bill $3755.00 for 16 days, and then got the rest cashed over to American dollars and up to Mike's room.

It was another lovely day, so they pushed Mike, bed and all outside again for an hour or more. He really loved that. Menno Epp stopped to say good bye and invited Mike back again sometime to give his testimony at their church. Mike said he would. Wendell called to say he would be down this PM and then stay overnight so we could all leave early next morning.

We are really all getting really excited.

Wendell arrived at the hospital about 4:30 and picked Paul and I up and took us out for supper. We really had a good time together. Wendell really shared some of his innermost feelings spiritual and physical. He was a real blessing to us. We then came back to the hospital and Paul, Wendell and Kerry Munroe and the Penner boy went out to where the cycles were stored so he would know where to pick them up.

While they were gone Fred and Elsie Gingrich stopped by the hospital to see us and surprise us and surprise us they did. Paul and Fred roomed together in college years ago and they live in Edmonton. He also pilots a plane so they flew down just to see us. How great. So when Jake came and picked us up at the hospital they went along too and got a motel room near Jake's home so we stayed at their motel room for a while so we could talk.

Fred and Wendell are in business together. Then about midnight Fred and Elsie walked with Paul and I back to the Weibe's and we had planned to stop for them in the morning and they were going to see us off at the airport and then leave for home too. They made this trip only to see us. How nice of them. Well, we got back to the Weibe's at midnight and they were still up waiting to talk a while too.

Well I was so excited about going home that I couldn't sleep anyway.

Anna had called that morning to say Dad was home but not good at all and wondering how soon we would be home. Well, PTL I could tell her the Lord willing we will be home midnight Tuesday night. Arnold Moshier also called to tell us what a great program they had at Mellinger's church Sunday night. Choraleers sang and they took a special offering for Mike and it amounted to $1200.00.

WOW! What excitement.

No wonder we couldn't sleep we were all excited about what God was doing for us. It all fit together like a puzzle.

Tuesday August 29

We were up early and had breakfast at 6:15. Jake, Elsie and children all got up to go along to see us off. We got over to the hospital and Doctor Dykstra had Mike all ready and strapped to the stretcher and the ambulance crew were there waiting to go.

We left the hospital at 7:00 and arrived at the airport around 7:45. Fred and Elsie were with us too. We watched them board Mike in the plane which wasn't easy for it was only an 8 passenger plane. They had to take out some seats to lay the stretcher on the floor.

Wendell's friend piloted the plane and then we had a co-pilot and then Wendell went along too and then Paul, Mike, Doctor Dykstra and myself.

The plane was full.

It was a perfect day, not a cloud in the sky and the sun shining brightly. I was praising the Lord from sun up to sun down that day. It was a smooth flight and we could see for miles. It was a two hour flight to Great Falls Montana. When we arrived there we had to go through customs from leaving Canada. No problem for Wendell had phoned ahead and explained our situation. An ambulance picked us up at the plane and taxied us into the terminal.

Then they carried Mike by stretcher to the plane and boarded him early.

We were in First Class and got treated as such. They couldn't have been nicer to us. We had to pay for 3 plane seats for Mike to cover the stretcher. Wendell arranged everything for us and when we went to pay him he would not take one cent for the tickets, time, phone calls, etc. Again the Lord blessed us and again I prayed Lord bless Wendell and Fred for their kind act of love.

We boarded Northwest Orient and headed for Chicago. We were late coming into Chicago but an ambulance was waiting for us and we had to pay for 3 hours lay over whether it was one hour or three hours. They were really super nice to us though for they gave us a conference room to wait in till they were ready for us to board. We were flying TWA into Harrisburg form Chicago. We got all the food and drinks we wanted for we were flying First Class all the way. We arrived in Harrisburg right on time and the boys were all there to meet us.

They were standing there on the other side of the fence crying and watching them load Mike into the Hershey ambulance.

Doctor Schwentker and Eileen Keegan were there to meet us too. This was Mike's doctor and nurse coordinator at Hershey Medical Center. I was really impressed that they did this.

Paul and I rode with the boys over to Hershey while Doctor Dykstra went with Mike in the ambulance. Again, we were there to see them unload Mike and the boys were so glad to see each other.

Mike had a big smile for all his brothers while all they could do for the moment was cry. Just so glad to see each other.

When they had Mike all settled in his room they left us all in his room for a short time. We all gathered around his bed joining hands and laying hands on Mike and we all prayed together. Mike seemed in good spirits and took the trip very well but was tired and again was in a whole new setting, another adjustment. PTL for a safe trip.

APPENDIX

Forewords in first printing of *Powered to Move*

Mike King's story is compelling; heart wrenching, uplifting, and soul searching. When 20 year old Mike King left his family home in Pennsylvania with his three friends for a cross country trip on their motorcycles, he had no idea that not only would his life change, but that the purpose for which he was created would be fulfilled as well. The motorcycle accident that severed his spine was devastating. As I read his account I cried. Mike's question became my question: "How could God allow this to happen to a young man in his prime with a lifetime of activity ahead of him?" I shared his anger, as I read about his hospital recovery with the painful, frustrating, humiliating changes in lifelong habits that had to be reset.

His doctor told him in a very stark conversation: "You will never walk again." It was the final blow. He was no longer a man. He was forever disabled, never to fulfill his dreams or pursue the career that his Dad had always dreamed of for him – managing the large and prosperous dairy farm, the pride of the family.

At first self-pity, isolation and depression dogged his pathway every day. There seemed to be no hope for him, no future, nothing but dependence, humiliation, and discouragement, but this is not the end of the story. His anger was channeled into pathways that he never would have trod had it not been for that fateful day in August of 1978. Not only did he regain his self-confidence and his physical ability to cope and excel, but also his faith was restored, and his anger turned to praise and worship. His challenges were great, but, as he says, "I just had to push through!"

When challenges affect any of us, we often ask, "Why me?" In Mike's case, he came to see that the REAL question was "Why NOT me?" That is a profound step that each of us must take as we travel through life. If you have not asked that question yet, you surely will.

As you read Powered to Move: The Mike King Story your life will change. There is no question that his experiences over the next 30 or more years following his injury will inspire you, challenge you, and encourage you. Whether you have a spinal injury, or are blind physically OR spiritually, or have some other disabling condition you were born with or that happened along the way, the life lessons Mike so eloquently shares came after deep sorrow, followed by exhilarating challenges like racing in the Boston Marathon and in other such events all over the world. He became a skier, and a coach, sang the national anthem at a big league ball game, and was a world traveler touching down in Africa, Europe, North and South America, and Asia. Each person's experience is different, but the pattern of God's handiwork in His children is always perfect.

I had many experiences working with and meeting hundreds of dedicated people who had fought for years, in some cases decades, to bring the issue of the disabled to the attention of policy makers at all levels of American society, so that unnecessary barriers could be removed. Thus all Americans would be on an equal footing for employment and access to public buildings. Compassion and care for our fellow man should be the norm, not the exception.

It was during this life-changing period of time in my life that I met Mike King. Mike had given up what he had been planning to do: take over his Dad's business of running the family Farm. He knew he couldn't manage the cattle, drive the equipment, or oversee the labor-intensive work on such a successful enterprise. So, what should he do? What could he do? After returning from a trip to Brazil with a friend he was having dinner with his Dad who casually asked him: "What are you going to do next?" Mike's response was: "I'm going to go across the country in my wheelchair." Thus was born The Challenge of a Lifetime. It turned out that two individuals had already crossed America in wheelchairs from the west to the east coast, so Mike was determined to travel from Alaska to Washington, DC. That had never been done before.

That began a series of exciting and challenging events that you will have to read about in Powered to Move: The Mike King Story, but that decision is what brought Mike King and Bob Sweet to a meeting on the steps of the U.S. Capitol building in Washington, DC after Mike had successfully traveled 5,605.8 miles in his wheelchair! I was asked by President Reagan to represent him and greet Mike on the occasion of his monumental achievement. It was my privilege and honor to meet Mike and congratulate him for his fortitude, his perseverance, and his faith in Jesus Christ that had motivated him to tell his story to thousands of others who NEEDED to hear the good news that just having a disability does not deter one from fulfilling the mission, the calling, and the life work that is unique to each individual.

Although the meeting was brief, and both Mike and I have continued on to fulfill the purposes for which we were created, I am honored and privileged to know him and to encourage you, the reader, to get to know him also by reading Powered to Move: The Mike King Story.

When Mike's Grandpa Zook softly whispered to Mike's Mom with his dying breath, he had it right:

"Tell Mike he's going to be alright."

You will get to know Mike the cyclist, the farmer, the college student, the paraplegic, the skier, the marathon racer, the coach, the world traveler, staff member for Joni Eareckson Tada, and husband of the love of his life, Sharyn. I was interested to note that not only did Mike become accomplished in these things; he also spent 20 years managing the family business! Isn't it amazing what God can do when we are surrendered to His will? Amazing indeed.

I hope your life will be impacted as deeply as mine was, both by meeting Mike in Washington, DC in August 1985, and by reading the draft copy of Powered to Move: The Mike King Story, at least three times!

You are in for a life changing experience!
Robert W. Sweet, Jr.
Chairman 1983-1989
The White House Working Group on Handicapped Policy

Postscript: On July 26, 1990 President George H.W. Bush signed into law the American's for Disability Act (ADA). The work of the White House Working Group on Handicapped Policy had laid the groundwork for this historic law, but there will always be more we can do to achieve complete equality for all disabled persons.

I agree wholeheartedly with Mike King:

"I long to accomplish a great and noble task, but it is my chief duty to accomplish small tasks as if they were great and noble. At the end of the race, at the end of the day, it isn't my story, it's HIS story."

The autobiography you are about to read introduces one of the most interesting lives you will ever encounter. Mike has been a personal friend since our trip together with *Joni and Friends* to China. His testimony touched my heart deeply then and continues to do so today. As professor of Bible at Dallas Theological Seminary, I occasionally ask guests to speak to our students in my *Job and Suffering* course. I have asked Mike to be one of our guests speakers. Your life will be deeply blessed by Mike's story. He has taken a tough, painful situation and redeemed it for the Lord's glory. Redeeming suffering is something only a life dedicated to the will of God can accomplish. Mike has turned his suffering into a ministry, redeeming the pain for the progress of the gospel.

Mike writes, "Imagine being 20 years old, strong and adventurous, with your whole life ahead of you, setting out on a cross-country motorcycle trip with three good friends. Picture the freedom, feel the wind on your face, visualize the beauty around you—until the moment a car pulls out in front of you; you're ejected from your bike and injured so severely no one expects you to live." So, his story begins. He ends with these words: "My physical capabilities changed in Calgary on August 13, 1978. My spiritual possibilities changed a year later. I began to believe my life had been spared for a purpose, and I decided to let God use me the best way He could." Mike King understood that Jesus Christ is King!

You will be presented with chapters like, "I Can Make It Through Anything" and "Sing to the Lord a New Song." He concludes with "Every Detail of Our Lives" is controlled by the Lord. Through his life story you will read how to overcome overwhelming obstacles, turn injury into identity, challenge yourself and others, face suffering with fearless faith, and be motivated to move personal mountains.

I recommend this book to athletes facing severe injury, pastors interested in disability ministry, persons facing disability personally or as care-givers, and individuals questioning the goodness of God. Mike's personal experiences will be not only helpful, but instructive and challenging.

Larry J. Waters, PhD
Dallas Theological Seminary